W9-BZN-248

REVIEW COPY
COURTESY OF
ENSLOW PUBLISHERS, INC

Charles Lindbergh

The People to Know Series

Madeleine Albright
0-7660-1143-7

Ansel Adams
0-7660-1847-4

Neil Armstrong
0-89490-828-6

Isaac Asimov
0-7660-1031-7

Robert Ballard
0-7660-1147-X

Margaret Bourke-White
0-7660-1534-3

Garth Brooks
0-7660-1672-2

Barbara Bush
0-89490-350-0

Willa Cather
0-89490-980-0

Bill Clinton
0-89490-437-X

Hillary Rodham Clinton
0-89490-583-X

Bill Cosby
0-89490-548-1

Walt Disney
0-89490-694-1

Bob Dole
0-89490-825-1

Marian Wright Edelman
0-89490-623-2

Bill Gates
0-89490-824-3

Ruth Bader Ginsberg
0-89490-621-6

John Glenn
0-7660-1532-7

Jane Goodall
0-89490-827-8

Al Gore
0-7660-1232-8

Tipper Gore
0-7660-1142-9

Billy Graham
0-7660-1533-5

Alex Haley
0-89490-573-2

Tom Hanks
0-7660-1436-3

Ernest Hemingway
0-89490-979-7

Ron Howard
0-89490-981-9

Steve Jobs
0-7660-1536-X

Helen Keller
0-7660-1530-0

John F. Kennedy
0-89490-693-3

Stephen King
0-7660-1233-6

John Lennon
0-89490-702-6

Maya Lin
0-89490-499-X

Charles Lindbergh
0-7660-1535-1

Jack London
0-7660-1144-5

Malcolm X
0-89490-435-3

Wilma Mankiller
0-89490-498-1

Branford Marsalis
0-89490-495-7

Anne McCaffrey
0-7660-1151-8

Barbara McClintock
0-89490-983-5

Rosie O'Donnell
0-7660-1148-8

Gary Paulsen
0-7660-1146-1

Christopher Reeve
0-7660-1149-6

Ann Richards
0-89490-497-3

Sally Ride
0-89490-829-4

Will Rogers
0-89490-695-X

Franklin D. Roosevelt
0-89490-696-8

Charles M. Schulz
0-7660-1846-6

Steven Spielberg
0-89490-697-6

John Steinbeck
0-7660-1150-X

Martha Stewart
0-89490-984-3

Amy Tan
0-89490-699-2

Alice Walker
0-89490-620-8

Andy Warhol
0-7660-1531-9

Simon Wiesenthal
0-89490-830-8

Elie Wiesel
0-89490-428-0

Frank Lloyd Wright
0-7660-1032-5

Charles Lindbergh

American Hero of Flight

Virginia Meachum

Enslow Publishers, Inc.

40 Industrial Road   PO Box 38
Box 398   Aldershot
Berkeley Heights, NJ 07922   Hants GU12 6BP
USA   UK

http://www.enslow.com

Copyright © 2002 by Virginia Meachum

All rights reserved.

No part of this book may be reproduced by any means
without the written permission of the publisher.

Library of Congress Cataloging-in-Publication Data

Meachum, Virginia.
    Charles Lindbergh : American hero of flight / by Virginia Meachum.
        p. cm. — (People to know)
    Includes bibliographical references and index.
    ISBN 0-7660-1535-1
    1. Lindbergh, Charles A. (Charles Augustus), 1902–1974—Juvenile literature.
    2. Air pilots—United States—Biography—Juvenile literature. [1. Lindbergh,
    Charles A. (Charles Augustus), 1902–1974. 2. Air pilots. 3. Spirit of St. Louis
    (Airplane) 4. Transatlantic flights.] I. Title. II. Series.
    TL540.L5 .M36 2001
    629.13'092—dc21
                                        2001001638
Printed in the United States of America

10 9 8 7 6 5 4 3 2 1

To Our Readers:
We have done our best to make sure all Internet Addresses in this book were active and
appropriate when we went to press. However, the author and the publisher have no control over and assume no liability for the material available on those Internet sites or on
other Web sites they may link to. Any comments or suggestions can be sent by e-mail
to comments@enslow.com or to the address on the back cover.

Every effort has been made to locate all copyright holders of material used in this
book. If any errors or omissions have occurred, corrections will be made in future
editions of this book.

Illustration Credits: Everett Collection, pp. 62, 71, 75, 87, 102; Lindbergh Picture
Collection, Manuscripts and Archives, Yale University Library, p. 14; Mary E. Schlecht,
p. 110; Minnesota Historical Society, pp. 17, 20, 23, 26, 35, 38, 94, 106; Missouri
Historical Society, St. Louis, pp. 6, 9, 41, 47, 55, 68; National Air and Space Museum,
Smithsonian Institution, pp. 44, 52, 64.

Cover Illustration: Library of Congress

Contents

Charles A. Lindbergh

A Pilot's Dream

By 1927, no pilot had ever flown alone nonstop across the Atlantic Ocean. Some had tried and failed, losing their lives in the attempt. But Charles A. Lindbergh, a twenty-five-year-old airmail pilot, was sure he could do it.

For several years, Raymond Orteig, a French-born American who owned a hotel in New York, offered a $25,000 prize to the first aviator to fly nonstop across the Atlantic from New York to Paris, or from Paris to New York. This spurred a number of flyers, both European and American, to enter the competition.[1]

Filled with a natural spirit for adventure, and confident of his flying ability, the unknown Lindbergh quietly began preparing to join the competition. In between doing his mail runs from St. Louis to

Chicago, he worked on his plan for a plane capable of long-distance flight. Then, after gaining financial backing from several St. Louis businessmen, he contracted with Ryan Airlines in San Diego to build his aircraft—a one-seat, single-engine monoplane (an airplane with one set of wings). When the plane was completed, Lindbergh flew the *Spirit of St. Louis* (named for his financial backers) on a test flight from San Diego to Curtiss Field, Long Island, near New York City. With one stop in St. Louis, his solo flight of less than twenty-two hours was the fastest that had ever been made from coast to coast. Charles Lindbergh had set a new transcontinental speed record.[2]

Ten days later, on May 20, 1927, the daring young pilot prepared to take off from Roosevelt Field, New York, enroute to Le Bourget Airfield near Paris—an air voyage spanning 3,600 miles.

Throughout the previous week, the route Lindbergh planned to follow to reach Paris had been covered with fog and storms. Finally, on May 19, the weather bureau reported clearing conditions over the ocean. Although rain and haze lingered over New York City, Lindbergh decided to begin his flight the next morning. Usually a sound sleeper, he could not relax the night before. Tossing and turning, he mentally reviewed his plans—the added weight of enough gasoline to cross the distance; the decision to not take a radio or a parachute because of their weight; the uncertainty of safe flying weather over the vast Atlantic Ocean. Dozing off and on, he finally got up, dressed, and went down to the hotel lobby. It was 2:45 A.M.[3]

In the predawn hours, Roosevelt Field was shrouded in mist and drizzle. Reporters, police, and spectators had gathered, slogging about in the mud. When Lindbergh arrived, he and his mechanics made a careful check of the *Spirit of St. Louis*. A total of 450 gallons of gasoline was loaded into the plane's five gasoline tanks. While the mechanics warmed up the engine, Lindbergh slipped his flying suit over his clothes, donned his helmet and goggles, and climbed into the cockpit. For food, he took along five sandwiches and two canteens of drinking water. He was

Before takeoff, Lindbergh gave the Spirit of St. Louis, *above, one last safety check.*

asked about taking only five sandwiches. "That's enough," he replied with a grin. "If I get to Paris I won't need any more. If I don't—well, I won't need any more either."[4]

Conditions were far from perfect. Due to muggy weather, the single engine was delivering less power than it should; the load was heavier than the *Spirit* had ever lifted before; the favored headwind from the east had suddenly changed to a tailwind; the rain-soaked runway would reduce his takeoff speed.[5] At that moment, he could still change his mind. But no, he was convinced it was time to start the flight.

Buckling his seat belt, he signaled the ground crew. The propeller was turned. The motor coughed, then fired. The blocks were pulled from in front of the wheels. With a wave and a smile, Lindbergh pushed the throttle forward to a roar and grasped the stick (the lever used to control the pitch and roll of an aircraft). The plane barely crept forward through the mud. Under each wing, a line of men pushed on the struts to move the plane along. As it gathered speed, the men fell behind, watching it become airborne. Would it rise high enough to clear the telephone wires at the end of the runway? It did—by twenty feet! The crowd cheered, and the *Spirit of St. Louis* faded into the mist beyond.

Newspapers reported Lindbergh flying over New England, then over Nova Scotia. Then he disappeared. No news by radio, no sightings by ships. The world waited anxiously.

Soaring hour after hour above the ocean, the silver plane battled fog, storms, and sleet. During the lonely night hours, its pilot battled a growing need for sleep. Eyes focused on the instrument panel, he dared not doze off. He could lose control and plunge into the sea. Lindbergh slapped his face sharply but hardly felt the blow. He shook his head, flexed his arms and legs, stamped his feet, and bounced up and down. Nothing helped. Then he poked his head out the window. Instantly an airstream from the propeller washed over his face, opened his eyes, and filled his lungs. Now he felt refreshed.[6]

Lindbergh had flown twenty-seven hours when he sighted black spots in the water. They were a fleet of fishing boats. This meant he was approaching land—the coast of Ireland. Wide awake now, he flew over southern England, crossed the English Channel, and followed the Seine River to Paris. It was nighttime as he circled the city's Eiffel Tower ablaze with lights. Guided by flares, he landed at Le Bourget Field. Suddenly, Lindbergh and his plane were engulfed by thousands of wildly cheering, jubilant Parisians.

And America was jubilant, too!

Lindbergh had conquered the distance. He had flown 3,600 miles, from New York to Paris, in 33 hours, 29 minutes. And he did it alone. Not only did he win the $25,000 Orteig Prize, but his courage and skill won the admiration of the world. Charles A. Lindbergh had become an American hero.

Boyhood—Farm and City

Charles Augustus Lindbergh was born on February 4, 1902, in Detroit, Michigan. His father, Charles August Lindbergh, known as C.A., had been born in Sweden and came to the United States with his parents as an infant. C.A. grew up to become a well-respected attorney and realtor in Little Falls, Minnesota. Young Charles's mother, Evangeline Land Lindbergh from Detroit, was a University of Michigan graduate, with a bachelor of science degree. She was teaching chemistry at Little Falls High School when she met her future husband. C.A., a widower with two young daughters, was seventeen years older than his second bride.

The Lindbergh home was a newly built, three-story frame house on 120 acres of farmland. Set on a bluff overlooking the Mississippi River, it was about two miles south of Little Falls. C.A.'s daughters were happy to be released from boarding school to live with their father and his new wife. The girls, Lillian and Eva, were fourteen and ten years old when Charles was born.

One Sunday afternoon in August 1905, a fire swept through the Lindbergh home. Charles's nurse rushed him several hundred yards away to the barn. "Charles, you *mustn't* watch!" she cried out. But as they rounded the corner of the barn, the three-year-old looked back. A column of black smoke rose from the top floor of the house.[1]

By the following day, only the stone-walled basement and brick chimney remained. C.A. immediately arranged to build a new home for his family, using the original basement as a foundation. While C.A. camped out on the farm to supervise the construction, Evangeline Lindbergh and the children moved into a hotel in Little Falls. In the fall, Lillian and Eva moved in with relatives in Little Falls and returned to school. Charles and his mother traveled by train to Detroit for a lengthy visit with her parents, Dr. Charles Henry Land and Evangeline Lodge Land, grandparents of young Charles.

By December 1905, C.A. had become so burdened with property taxes, and with debts on land investments, that plans for the new house had to be scaled back. There was a first floor, an unfinished second floor, and a partially screened-in back porch overlooking the Mississippi. Charles claimed the porch as his bedroom. This was where he would spend all but the coldest nights, sleeping on a folding cot, "in close contact with sun, wind, rain and stars," he later wrote.[2]

Living on the farm, Charles had little contact with children his own age. Outdoors most of the time, he was surrounded by farm animals and he always had a dog as a companion.

One summer afternoon, while Charles was upstairs polishing stones he had collected along the river, the sound of a motor drew him to the window and onto the porch roof. Less than two hundred yards away, he saw an airplane flying above the treetops.

Charles, age six, with his mother, Evangeline Land Lindbergh.

It was a biplane, with two sets of wings, one above the other, and a pilot perched between in a box. Charles raced downstairs to tell his mother. She explained that an aviator had come to Little Falls to give rides to anyone who dared fly with him. She said it was very dangerous and expensive.[3]

The sight of that airplane fueled Charles's imagination. Sometimes he would imagine himself with wings, "swooping off the roof into the valley, and then soaring into the air above the tops of trees."[4]

By 1906, C.A. Lindbergh had become active in politics. He supported farmers and small businesses. He opposed high interest rates charged on farm loans by eastern bankers. In November 1907, he was elected Republican congressman from Minnesota's Sixth District.

Each fall, Charles and his mother followed his father by train to Washington, D.C. On the way, they stopped in Detroit to visit his grandfather and grandmother Land. Arriving in Washington later, they stayed in a furnished apartment until Congress adjourned in the spring. Then Charles and his mother would stop again in Detroit on the way back to Little Falls.

In the summer of 1909, when Charles was seven years old, his parents' marriage fell apart. They had quarreled frequently—mostly about finances. Evangeline Lindbergh wanted a divorce. C.A. knew that the conservative farm families in his district would not approve of a divorced congressman.[5]

Neither C.A. nor his wife seemed capable of showing affection, but both cared deeply for their son. They agreed to stay married but to live apart. Charles and his mother would spend winters in Washington near C.A.'s office. In the summer, they would return to the farm. C.A. would live in Minneapolis or with relatives in Little Falls.[6] There was never a formal separation. Charles was merely told that from then on, he would live with his mother, but he would see his father frequently.[7]

In Washington, Charles spent hours in his father's office or with him in the halls of the House of Representatives. Once he accompanied his father to the White House and was introduced to President Woodrow Wilson. He was not afraid, he said later, because "the President was just a man even if he is President."[8]

Evangeline Lindbergh took Charles to places of interest in and around the nation's capital. At Fort Myer, Virginia, Charles attended his first air meet. He recalled this experience as "so intense and fascinating that I wanted to fly myself."[9] On January 4, 1913, C.A. sent Charles and his mother on a voyage to Panama to see the canal under construction. Charles's father considered these experiences an "educational advantage" over living year-round in Little Falls.[10]

Each spring when Congress adjourned, Charles looked forward to visiting his grandparents in Detroit. Dr. Land was both a dentist and an inventor. He perfected a method of making porcelain crowns for decayed teeth and wrote two books on dentistry. He invented high-temperature gas and oil burners, and an air-conditioning system for his home. His

Charles with his father, C.A. Lindbergh, who was a congressman in Washington, D.C.

basement laboratories and his ability to make or fix anything with his hands impressed young Charles.[11]

Summers on the farm, Charles found much to do. From an early age, he kept busy building things—a pair of wooden stilts, a raft to pole himself through Mississippi streams, a lookout platform ten feet above the ground in a tree.

He was also interested in mechanical things. Once, Martin Engstrom, a hardware merchant from Little Falls, came to the farm to repair a motor-driven pump. He was surprised to find Charles so knowledgeable about pumps and motors. The nine-year-old had figured out why the pump was not working.[12]

C.A. visited the farm often. He taught Charles to fish, hike, hunt, pitch a tent, and paddle a canoe. He taught him to swim by stressing self-reliance. C.A. often swam, carrying Charles on his back, to an island rock in the Mississippi River. One day Charles waded out, accidentally slipped into a hole, and went under. When he surfaced, frantically splashing and paddling, his father was standing on the rock laughing. Then Charles realized that he was swimming by himself.[13]

In the summer of 1912, C.A. bought a Model T Ford. The car had to be started with a hand crank, and the gears were shifted with a foot pedal. Learning to drive was a struggle for both parents, often sending them into a fence or a ditch. Many times they arrived in town with the radiator steaming.[14]

Charles was permitted to drive on the farm, though he could barely see over the steering wheel.

By the following summer, he had grown taller and drove his mother on trips to nearby towns.

For the spring primary election of 1916, C.A. decided not to seek a sixth term as a congressman but to run for the United States Senate instead. He traded in the Ford for a new Saxon sedan, and fourteen-year-old Charles chauffeured his father during the campaign. Unhappily, C.A. Lindbergh was defeated in his bid for the Senate. He returned to Washington to finish out the remaining months of his congressional term.[15]

Meanwhile, Evangeline Lindbergh planned a trip to California. Charles would drive, and then enroll in a California high school for his junior year.

In August 1916, Charles, his mother, and her brother Charles started out for the West Coast. The trip was brutal. Heavy rainstorms turned unpaved roads into sludge. Often they had to stay in a local hotel for days until the roads dried out. After forty days, they arrived in California.[16]

Uncle Charles returned by train to Detroit. Young Charles and his mother rented a cottage in Redondo Beach, and he enrolled in Redondo Union High School. In April, when they learned that Grandmother Land had been diagnosed with cancer, Charles drove his mother back to Little Falls.

That fall, Charles and his mother prepared for their first winter on the farm. Grandmother Land would be living with them during the final stage of her illness. The house needed to be winterized—a furnace installed and indoor plumbing and other necessities added. C.A. financed the improvements, but the

Charles had few friends, but he always had a dog to pal around with on the family farm. Dingo was one of his favorites.

duties of a homeowner fell upon fifteen-year-old Charles. He was enrolled in Little Falls High School for his senior year.

Charles's father did not have much respect for formal education. He did not think healthy youngsters should be cooped up in a classroom.[17]

Evangeline Lindbergh's habit of stopping in Detroit on the way to and from Washington meant Charles started school late and withdrew before the school year ended. As a result, he was behind in his studies. By the age of sixteen, Charles had attended eleven schools, and none for a full academic year.[18]

That year at Little Falls High School, Charles began to excel in subjects that interested him— physics and mechanical drawing. But a heavy workload at home left little time for study. Finding a tenant to run the farm had not been possible, so Charles was handling the work. Meanwhile, his grades were falling and his chances of graduating looked slim.[19]

By 1917, the United States was actively involved in World War I. Many farm workers had been drafted into the army, and food production was becoming scarce. Early in 1918, the high school principal announced that senior boys who dropped out of school to work on a farm would graduate automatically. Charles left school immediately to work full-time on his father's farm.

On June 5, 1918, he returned to Little Falls High School to receive his diploma.[20]

3

Eye on the Sky

With Charles excused from high school studies, C.A. decided his farm should go into full production. He could not farm himself because of other business interests, so he put sixteen-year-old Charles in charge of the 120 acres. A retired lumberjack, Daniel Thompson, was hired to live in the tenants' house and help around the farm.

C.A. ordered a carload of cattle and sheep. Then he gave Charles authority to buy whatever machinery was needed for plowing and harvesting. Determined to use modern methods, Charles ordered a tractor, a gangplow, a disc harrow, and a seeder.[1]

Charles became a full-time farmer. He worked long hours in the fields with the tractor. He built a silo for winter feeding and installed one of the first milking machines in the county.[2]

By the following year, with the farm running smoothly, he began to think about his future. Ever since attending his first air show at Fort Myer, Virginia, he had been fascinated with flying.[3] Charles wanted to become an aviator. He planned to enlist in the Army Air Corps the moment he was old enough. But his plan vanished on November 11, 1918. The armistice was signed, ending World War I and the immediate need for pilots.

Charles farmed for another year. He also bought himself a twin-cylinder Excelsior motorcycle, which he rode through town and country at daredevil speeds.[4] In the spring of 1919, he was ready to quit farming. The work was hard, repetitious, and sometimes dangerous. One evening in May, as he was turning the tractor at the field's edge, a steel blade

As a teenager, Charles liked to speed through the streets on his Excelsior motorcycle.

passed within inches of his head and crashed to the ground. If he had not been turning the tractor at that moment, he would have been crushed by the gang-plow as it flipped over.[5]

Once again he began to plan his future. As college graduates, his parents favored a college education for their son. He decided to study mechanical engineering at the University of Wisconsin in Madison. In the spring of 1920, he turned the farm over to tenants, in preparation to leave.

When Charles decided to enroll at the University of Wisconsin, his mother revived her teaching career. She got a job teaching science at a junior high school in Madison and rented a third-floor apartment for the two of them near the university. The money she earned was needed because they were receiving less financial help from C.A. He had lost money in real estate deals, political campaigns, and a magazine venture, *Lindbergh's National Farmer.*[6]

Charles rode his motorcycle 350 miles from Little Falls to Madison to enroll. He soon became friends with two engineering school classmates who also owned motorcycles. Richard Plummer was a studious youth who enjoyed hunting and fishing. Delos Dudley was the son of the university's assistant librarian, Professor W. H. Dudley.[7] For recreation, the three friends traveled around the Madison countryside on their motorcycles.

Charles did not participate in campus social life. He showed no interest in girls, had never learned to dance, and did not date while at the university. The one campus activity that appealed to him was the Reserve Officer Training Corps (ROTC). He became a member of both the rifle and pistol teams.

Charles believed in keeping physically fit. He neither drank or smoked. He gave up coffee when he joined the rifle team, convinced that caffeine reduced the steadiness of his hand and eye. In 1921, thanks to his ability to score fifty bull's-eyes in a row in shooting matches, he took the lead as the best shot on the team.[8]

That summer, continuing his ROTC commitment, Lindbergh rode his Excelsior to Camp Knox (later known as Fort Knox), Kentucky, for six weeks of field artillery training. He enjoyed the daily ritual, the physical challenges, the discipline, and the comradeship of the other cadets.[9]

Returning to the Madison campus in the fall, he showed little enthusiasm for academic classes. In the first half of his sophomore year, his record was so poor that the Adviser Committee recommended he be dropped from the university.[10]

This was more of a disappointment to Evangeline Lindbergh than to her son. Now he could do what he had always wanted to do—learn to fly. When Lindbergh told his parents that he wanted to quit school and become a pilot, his father said, "Flying is too dangerous and you're my only son."[11] His mother said, "If you really want to fly, that's what you should do."[12]

At the end of March 1922, Lindbergh dropped out of the University of Wisconsin and headed for Lincoln,

Charles did not study very much at the University of Wisconsin.

Nebraska, on his motorcycle. There he would become a student at the Nebraska Aircraft Corporation.

He arrived at the factory on April 3, and met the corporation president, Ray Page. Lindbergh was charged $500 to study at the "school." There were no other paying students, but there were pilots and mechanics who could teach flying and maintenance. Tall and slender, Lindbergh became known as "Slim" by the factory workers and pilots.

The Nebraska Aircraft Corporation was in the business of buying old army training planes and converting them to civilian use. The Lincoln Standard was a biplane, with two open cockpits, one in back for the pilot and a two-passenger cockpit in front.[13]

Lindbergh was intrigued with everything about the factory: the 150-horsepower engines, the wooden struts, the pairs of fragile wings waiting to be bound to the fuselages. He watched the workmen closely, helping when needed, and learned about aeronautical theory and airplane design.[14]

After one week at the factory, Lindbergh experienced his first airplane flight. A new Lincoln Standard had just been assembled and hauled onto the field for a final checkup by the engineer and the mechanic. Lindbergh and a sixteen-year-old handyman, Harlan (Bud) Gurney, were invited to climb into the front cockpit for a test run. Belted down, goggles and leather helmets in place, they watched every detail unfold.[15]

"Contact!" Otto Timm, the pilot, called out. At the plane's nose, a mechanic jerked down on the propeller. The motor coughed, then roared. The spinning propeller became a blur; the entire plane vibrated. Quieting the motor, the pilot nodded for the men standing by to remove the blocks from in front of the wheels. With motor roaring, the plane moved forward, bumping over the field faster and faster. Then, lifting, it climbed upward and leveled off. The houses and fields below looked small and neat, like squares on a checkerboard. As wind whipped their cheeks and wisps of cloud sped past, Gurney and Lindbergh looked at each other, grinning. Later, back on the ground, Lindbergh knew he had found his true career. The excitement even surpassed the thrills of motorcycling.[16]

Ira Biffle was to be Lindbergh's instructor. An instructor with the Army Signal Corps during the war, Biffle was known for his toughness. After seeing a good friend killed in a plane crash, he had lost his love of flying. Biffle found the slightest excuses to postpone in-flight instruction. Often he would not show up at all.[17]

After six weeks, Lindbergh had received only eight hours of flight instruction. He had learned to take off and land. Now he was ready to fly alone—to solo. But Ray Page had just sold the company's training plane. He would not allow Lindbergh to use another plane unless he put up a cash bond to cover possible damage. Lindbergh did not have enough cash for a bond. He also did not have enough flying hours to apply for a pilot's job, even if he did solo.[18]

What should he do? Erold G. Bahl, a barnstorming pilot, had purchased Page's training plane. Lindbergh asked Bahl if he needed a helper during his next barnstorming tour, and offered to pay his own expenses. Bahl accepted the offer.[19]

Barnstorming is the aviator's term for flying from town to town to perform stunts in the air. Then the pilots would offer short flights to anyone interested. In 1922, the usual charge was $5 for a five- or ten-minute ride.[20]

On the tour, Lindbergh suggested that he wing-walk to draw a bigger crowd. In wing-walking, a flyer steps out of the front cockpit while the plane is in flight, then walks onto the lower wing of the plane.

When Bahl swooped down over a town, Lindbergh stood on the wing and gained instant attention. The stunt drew a bigger crowd wherever the plane landed, with more people eager to pay for a ride. Now Bahl could afford to pay Lindbergh's expenses. They returned to Lincoln in June, and Lindbergh did odd jobs at the factory. He was saving to buy his own plane.

Later in June, parachute-maker Charles Hardin stopped at the factory to sell his product. Lindbergh watched him demonstrate a jump. Two thousand feet above the field, Hardin fell off the wing of a plane. His white parachute opened and he drifted to the ground. Lindbergh wanted to have that experience.[21] But he wanted to do a double jump. In a double jump, one chute opens and is discarded. A second one opens and delivers the jumper to the ground.[22]

After receiving instructions from Hardin, Lindbergh borrowed two parachutes, and at eighteen hundred feet he made his jump. The first chute opened perfectly. He cut it loose and waited for the second one to open. It seemed to take much longer, and Lindbergh began to fall headfirst. At last the parachute opened, carrying him down to a rough landing.[23]

Later, Lindbergh learned how close he had come to death. The break cord between the two chutes had snapped too soon. Hardin, having no cord on hand, had tied the two chutes together with a piece of rotting grocery string.[24]

In mid-July 1922, Harold J. Lynch, an experienced pilot, invited Lindbergh to come on a barnstorming tour as a mechanic, wing-walker, and parachute jumper. The factory still owed Lindbergh two more hours of instruction. He traded his claim to that, and threw in an additional $25 cash, for a new parachute. Storing his motorcycle in the factory basement, he joined Lynch for the summer.

They flew over the Midwest. Lindbergh was billed as "DAREDEVIL LINDBERGH" on the leaflets they dropped over towns. "People came for miles to watch me climb back and forth over wings, and finally leap off into space," Lindbergh recalled. "I lived in a world of clouds and sky."[25]

The barnstorming season ended in October, and Lindbergh picked up his motorcycle at the factory. He rode to Detroit to see his mother, who was now teaching science at Cass Technical High School. Then he went on to Minneapolis to spend the winter with his father.

Flying High

While visiting with his father during the winter, Lindbergh talked of little else besides airplanes. Convinced of his son's determination to become a pilot, C.A. signed a note at the bank for Lindbergh to borrow enough cash to purchase a plane.[1]

In March 1923, Lindbergh traveled to Souther Field, Georgia. At this former wartime training field, the U.S. Army was selling off surplus World War I planes. Lindbergh selected a Jenny, for which he paid $500. The name Jenny came from the initials of the plane, the Curtiss JN-4D. The price included a new engine, installation of an extra twenty-gallon gasoline tank, and a fresh coat of olive-drab dope—a material used to strengthen the fabric surface. This biplane with dual controls had a top speed of seventy-five miles an hour.[2]

It was time for Lindbergh to take off in his very own airplane. He had never soloed. In 1923, a license was not required to fly, and it was assumed at the airfield that he was an experienced pilot.

Lindbergh taxied to the end of the field, but on takeoff he skidded on a wing and a wheel. A stranger, waiting for delivery of his own plane, offered to climb in and instruct him on takeoffs and landings. After several successful landings, he assured Lindbergh he would have no trouble. That evening, when the air was still, Lindbergh made his first solo flight.

This was a high point in his dream of flying. "To be absolutely alone for the first time in the cockpit of a plane hundreds of feet above ground is an experience never to be forgotten," Lindbergh recalled.[3]

After a week of practice flights, he took off for Minnesota. He planned to earn cash along the way by taking passengers aloft. On his second day out, an oncoming storm forced Lindbergh to land in a pasture. As he taxied toward a grove of trees where he intended to tie the plane down, his plane dropped into a ditch and splintered the propeller. This was his first "crack-up."[4]

Having heard the noise, a crowd of neighbors gathered, and Lindbergh was given a ride into the nearest town, Maben, Mississippi. He wired Souther Field for a new propeller, then settled into the local hotel. When the new propeller arrived, Lindbergh installed it, made a test flight, and then persuaded one of the curious onlookers to take a ride. Others followed. Two weeks later, he departed with $250 more than when he had arrived.[5]

Lindbergh flew north, often challenged by high winds, electrical storms, and the need for a safe place to land. When the weather cleared, his plane always drew a curious crowd, eager for a $5 ride in the sky.

His destination was Shakopee, Minnesota, where he planned to meet his father and fly him around on the final weeks of his campaign tour. Minnesota's senior senator Knute Nelson had recently died, and the vacancy was to be filled by a special election. C.A. wanted to try for the office.[6]

Shortly before reaching Shakopee, Lindbergh was forced down by a severe storm. Again the propeller was damaged, and another had to be ordered and installed. He caught up with his father in Marshall, Minnesota, where C.A. climbed into the cockpit for his first airplane ride. From then on, Lindbergh never heard a word against his flying, and his father never missed a chance to ride in the plane.[7] When the campaign was over, however, C.A. lost the election.

During the summer of 1923, Lindbergh barnstormed around Minnesota and Wisconsin. In midsummer, Evangeline Lindbergh met her son at Janesville, Minnesota, and barnstormed with him for ten days through central Minnesota. It was a pleasant time for both of them.[8]

By fall, with colder weather, few people wanted to ride in an open cockpit. Lindbergh flew south to attend the International Air Races at Lambert Field in St. Louis, Missouri.

Lambert was crowded with modern planes, and Lindbergh had to park his small craft a mile away on a hilly pasture. Walking around the field, examining the many types of planes, and mixing with so many sophisticated pilots, Lindbergh became aware of his second-class status. His Jenny was among the slowest aircraft.[9]

Lindbergh sold the Jenny. He stayed around Lambert for the winter giving flying lessons. He had more than two hundred flying hours to his credit, and a teaching certificate was not required at that time.[10]

While at Lambert, he met Marvin Northrop, the owner of a small aircraft manufacturing firm near St. Louis. When Northrop learned about Lindbergh's flying experience, he urged him to sign up with the U.S. Army as an air cadet. He would have an opportunity to learn the technical details of flying, and to fly some of the newer type planes. That night, Lindbergh wrote to Washington for an application.[11]

To support himself while waiting for his application to be processed, Lindbergh continued giving flying lessons and occasionally barnstormed with another pilot. In January 1924, he passed the army entrance examinations at Chanute Field in Rantoul, Illinois. Soon after, he received orders to appear at Brooks Field in San Antonio, Texas, to enlist as a flying cadet.[12]

On March 15, 1924, at the age of twenty-two, Lindbergh was one of 104 cadets entering the yearlong training program of the Army Air Service School. The study program was difficult. It included twenty-four ground-school courses, with frequent written exams—some as long as eight hours. After the first exam session, Cadet Lindbergh was only one point away from being dropped from the program. This shocked him into studying harder.[13] Lindbergh remembered this critical time: "I began studying as I had never studied before—evenings, weekends, sometimes in the washroom after bed check, far into the night."[14]

Less than a month after Lindbergh's enlistment, he received word that his father was critically ill with a brain tumor. Lindbergh was granted a ten-day leave, and he traveled by train to the Mayo Clinic in Rochester, Minnesota, where C.A. was a patient. By

Lindbergh adjusts his parachute before taking off from Lambert Field in 1925.

now his father could no longer speak, but he recognized his son. Silently, they held hands.[15] On May 24, 1924, C.A. Lindbergh died. His body was cremated. Later, Lindbergh would fly over the family home in Minnesota and scatter his father's ashes.[16]

Lindbergh's final months of training included formation flying, bombing, strafing, gunnery, and photography. His was the first class to be issued parachutes, and that proved to be fortunate.

Nine days before graduation, Lindbergh was involved in an in-flight accident. During mock-attack maneuvers, Cadet Phil Love was in the lead plane, and Lieutenant C. D. McAllister's and Lindbergh's planes were flying side by side. Suddenly the wings of the two planes locked together. As the planes began spinning, each man jumped backward from his aircraft and parachuted to safety.[17]

For this emergency jump, Lindbergh and McAllister became members twelve and thirteen of the Caterpillar Club—men who had parachuted from airplanes to save their lives. (The club was named after the insect that created the raw silk used to make the cloth for parachutes.)[18]

The following week, on March 14, 1925, only nineteen cadets graduated out of the 104 who had started one year before. They were commissioned as second lieutenants in the Air Service Reserve Corps. Charles A. Lindbergh was the top man in his class.[19]

Additional pilots were not needed by the Army Air Service at this time, but the graduates would remain members of the Air Service Reserve Corps. Lindbergh boarded a train for St. Louis to see what civilian jobs might be available. Within days he was offered a job by Robertson Aircraft Corporation.

Congress had passed the "Kelly Bill" on February 2, 1925, authorizing the United States Post Office to award airmail contracts to private companies. Robertson Aircraft Corporation, co-owned by William and Frank Robertson, had bid on the Chicago–St. Louis route. Impressed with Lindbergh when he had been barnstorming out of Lambert Field, they offered him the position of chief airmail pilot.[20]

While waiting for the government contract to arrive, Lindbergh enlisted in the Missouri National Guard. He lectured to wartime pilots on navigation, parachuting, and other techniques he had learned at Brooks Field. He was promoted to first lieutenant and later to the rank of captain.[21]

By April 1926, Robertson Aircraft Corporation had received the government contract to establish the Chicago–St. Louis airmail route. Lindbergh's job as chief pilot was to select two other pilots and supervise operations of the route. He hired former army buddies Phil Love and Thomas Nelson. The three pilots were to make a total of five round trips a week in De Havilland observation planes that had been purchased from the army and rebuilt. In these biplanes, which cruised at about ninety miles an hour, the pilot sat in the back cockpit and the mail sacks were carried in the front one. Lindbergh specified that each pilot must be equipped with a parachute for emergency use.[22]

On April 15, 1926, Lindbergh flew the first south-bound airmail from Chicago's airfield, in suburban

Maywood, to St. Louis. The trip took two and three-quarter hours, with stops in Peoria and Springfield, Illinois.[23]

Airmail pilots flew in all kinds of weather, day or night. The routes were not lighted and weather reports were unreliable. Sometimes a pilot's only landing light was the flashlight he carried in his belt. In fog or sleet, pilots flew as far as they could, then landed and sent the mail on by train. Lindbergh was forced to parachute four times from planes disabled by storms or engine failure. He was never injured, but his main concern was locating the wreckage and recovering the mailbags to be forwarded by train.[24]

Flying the mail was full of risks, testing a pilot's courage and skill. But for Lindbergh, it provided the challenges on which he seemed to thrive.

Piloting a plane was always risky. Lindbergh's airmail plane went down more than once. This crash took place near Chicago in October 1926.

5

A Major Challenge

The idea of a New York–Paris flight first came to Lindbergh in the fall of 1926. While flying the mail from St. Louis to Chicago, he began thinking about the challenge offered by New York hotel owner Raymond Orteig. The Orteig Prize—$25,000 to the first aviator to fly nonstop between New York and Paris—made headlines each time an attempt was made. So far, each pilot had failed.

The latest attempt had occurred on September 15, 1926. French air ace René Fonck had come to the United States to compete for the prize. His three-engine biplane was equipped with upholstered red-leather seats, a convertible sofa bed, long- and short-wave radio sets, and other comforts. With a crew of four, his plane taxied down New York's

Roosevelt Field runway but failed to lift off. Crashing over a twenty-foot embankment, it exploded and burned. Fonck and his navigator escaped. The radio operator and mechanic lost their lives.[1]

Reading about this tragedy, Lindbergh visualized how he would plan a New York–Paris flight. First he would eliminate all the extra weight—the three engines, the sofa bed, and the four-man crew. He would fly a single-engine plane with a Wright Whirlwind engine, and he would fly alone. A solo flight would be less expensive and would allow the pilot to make all the decisions.[2]

Lindbergh was convinced that he could make a successful transatlantic flight if he had the right plane. But the right plane would be costly, and he had saved only $2,000. He needed financial backers—people as enthusiastic about the flight as he.

For the next few months, Lindbergh spent every spare minute between airmail duties trying to per-suade St. Louis businessmen to support his New York–Paris plan. Why should they support his plan? A successful flight "would show people what airplanes can do," he told them. "It would advance aviation, and it would advertise St. Louis."[3]

Major Albert B. Lambert, for whom the St. Louis airfield was named, was the first to listen to Lindbergh's plan. He volunteered $1,000. Two more men joined the project—Harry H. Knight, president of the St. Louis Flying Club, and Harold M. Bixby, pres-ident of the St. Louis Chamber of Commerce. Others added their support. Lindbergh now had a group of backers and $15,000, including his own $2,000.[4]

Lindbergh was certain that he could fly across the Atlantic Ocean if he had the right aircraft.

Next he needed to find the right plane. Ryan Airlines, a little-known company in San Diego, seemed to meet all of his requirements.

In February 1927, Lindbergh traveled to San Diego. He met with the owner of Ryan Airlines, Benjamin Franklin Mahoney, and the chief engineer, Donald Hall.

In discussing design, Lindbergh said he would need only one cockpit. "You don't plan on making that flight alone, do you?" asked Hall. Lindbergh said he would be better off with extra gasoline than with an extra man.[5]

Instantly, Hall saw the advantage of a solo flight. Only one cockpit would mean a shorter, lighter fuselage, which would allow the plane to carry several more gallons of fuel. Hall estimated that such a plane could fly at least four thousand miles. Mahoney figured a price of $10,580 for the plane, including a Wright engine.

Lindbergh wired his St. Louis backers to sign a contract with Ryan Airlines. Approval from St. Louis came the next day. Immediately, Hall and Lindbergh began working together on the design.[6]

Two months of intensive labor followed, with Lindbergh making the final decisions. Reducing weight was uppermost in those decisions. His own weight of 170 pounds was considered. His pilot's seat would be a cut-down wicker chair. To allow for his six-foot-plus height, a hollowed area was cut out above his head in the cabin. The cockpit would be placed behind the main fuel tank. This would block Lindbergh's forward view, but it would provide a safety advantage. In the event of a crack-up, he would not be crushed between the engine and the gasoline tank. He could see ahead by periscope or by banking the plane. Not carrying a parachute or a radio reduced the plane's weight enough to allow for even more gasoline.[7]

Construction became a race against time. In early March, news wires reported that Commander Richard Byrd was planning a May transatlantic flight. René Fonck, despite his previous tragedy, was planning a flight in his new plane. Commander Noel Davis's biplane was scheduled for an Atlantic crossing in June.[8]

The factory work on Lindbergh's plane was completed on April 25, with the name *Spirit of St. Louis* painted on each side of the silver plane's nose.

The *Spirit* was built of spruce wood, steel tubing, piano wire, and cotton fabric. The fabric had been made airtight and watertight with a coat of dope. The gasoline tanks had a total capacity of 450 gallons. At a speed averaging one hundred miles an hour, the *Spirit* promised to fly more than four thousand miles nonstop.[9]

Lindbergh's application as a contestant for the Orteig Prize had been accepted by the National Aeronautic Association. The Aeronautics Division of the United States Department of Commerce issued license number N-X 211 for the *Spirit of St. Louis*, as well as a new pilot's license for Lindbergh.[10]

On May 10, 1927, at 3:55 P.M., he took off in the *Spirit of St. Louis* for Lambert Field. He arrived the following morning at 6:20 A.M. The flight had set a

The instrument panel on the Spirit of St. Louis: *Lindbergh could not see out of the plane except by periscope or by leaning out the side windows.*

new speed record of fourteen hours and twenty-five minutes from the West Coast.[11]

The next morning, May 12, Lindbergh took off for New York. Seven hours and twenty minutes later, he landed at Curtiss Field on Long Island, New York. He had crossed the entire country in less than twenty-two hours, setting another record.[12]

Airport manager Casey Jones provided a hangar for Lindbergh's plane. Dick Blythe, a public relations man from Wright Aeronautical Corporation, escorted

Lindbergh to the nearby Garden City Hotel, where he would stay until departing for Paris. All of the competing pilots—Clarence Chamberlin, Commander Byrd, and Lindbergh—were using Wright Corporation engines. Dick Blythe was assigned to handle press relations for all three pilots.[13]

Until then, the aeronautical news had centered on the recent flight attempts of Lindbergh's competitors. Early in April, Commander Byrd's trimotor Fokker crashed on a test flight. On April 24, Clarence Chamberlin's Wright-Bellanca plane lost part of its landing gear during takeoff and made a crash landing. Two days later during a trial flight, Commander Noel Davis and Lieutenant Stanton Wooster crashed into a marshland and lost their lives. Also, the world anxiously waited for news of Captains Charles Nungesser and François Coli. On May 8, the two French war aces had taken off in their biplane from Le Bourget Airfield near Paris, heading to New York. Five days later, they still had not been sighted.[14]

Now the press centered its attention on Captain Charles Lindbergh—the twenty-five-year-old pilot who was planning a solo flight to Paris. "FLYING FOOL HOPS TODAY" read one headline. Actually, the weather was so unfavorable, Lindbergh had no intention of "hopping" that day.[15]

Among the people who went to see Lindbergh was Harry F. Guggenheim, president of the Daniel Guggenheim Fund for the Promotion of Aeronautics. He inspected the *Spirit*, sat in Lindbergh's cramped cockpit, and wished him luck. But all the while he was thinking, "He'll never make it."[16]

All week, Lindbergh and the two other contenders, Byrd and Chamberlin, had been waiting for the fog and storms across the coast of North America to clear. On the night of May 19, on the way to a theater performance, Lindbergh phoned the New York Weather Bureau. To his surprise, the prediction was for clearing along the coast. Immediately he returned to Curtiss Field and ordered his plane to be readied for an early-morning flight.[17] Neither Byrd nor Chamberlin seemed to be preparing for a takeoff.

It was after midnight when Lindbergh went to bed at the hotel, but he slept very little. By the time he arrived on the field at daybreak, he had been awake for twenty-three hours. Facing him was a thirty-six-hundred-mile flight, alone.[18]

The field was alive with spectators, police, and newsmen. A movie crew from the Fox Film Corporation had arrived to record the first newsreel ever taken with sound.[19]

On Friday, May 20, 1927, at 7:52 A.M., Lindbergh climbed into the cockpit and revved up the engine. The fuel tank blocked his forward view, so he leaned out the left-side window to see the narrow, muddy runway. With the throttle wide open, his plane lumbered forward, like an overloaded truck. Flight seemed doubtful. But then the *Spirit* bounced, skimmed a puddle, and took to the air. Barely rising above the telephone wires in its path, it flew away, soon beyond view. Charles Lindbergh and the *Spirit of St. Louis* were on their way to Paris! Said one reporter who was at the scene, "Five hundred onlookers believed they had witnessed a miracle."[20]

Lindbergh standing beside the Spirit of St. Louis. *"Flying Fool Hops Today" read one newspaper headline before he took off for Paris.*

Lindbergh's course took him over Nova Scotia, Newfoundland, east across the Atlantic, south past Ireland and England, and on to Paris.[21]

Beyond Newfoundland lay almost two thousand miles of ocean. Lindbergh battled storms, fog, sleet, and sleep. In the thirty-third hour of flight, over Deauville, France, Lindbergh had flown thirty-five hundred miles—breaking the world's distance record for a nonstop airplane flight. He reached into the paper bag next to his seat for a sandwich. It was his first food since takeoff.[22]

Shortly after 10:00 P.M., on May 21, Lindbergh circled Le Bourget Airport. He was puzzled by the enormous traffic jams on nearby roads. What Lindbergh did not know was that after he was sighted over Cherbourg, France, word of his approach had reached Paris by telephone and telegraph. All of Paris seemed headed for the airfield to greet him.[23]

Almost before the *Spirit*'s propeller stopped, both Lindbergh and his plane were engulfed by thousands of cheering Parisians. He would have cheered, too, but he was concerned for his plane, which began to crack from the pressure of the crowd. Stepping from the cockpit, he was seized by dozens of hands and carried on top of the joyful throng. Several French military aviators saw his plight and took action. They snatched his helmet and placed it on the head of an American reporter. "Here is Lindbergh!" they shouted. At once, the reporter became the center of attention and the real Lindbergh was freed.[24]

The aviators whisked Lindbergh off to meet U.S. ambassador Myron T. Herrick. Meanwhile, the *Spirit of St. Louis* was surrounded by guards and later placed in a hangar.

Lindbergh was unprepared for the worldwide interest his landing in Paris caused. He stayed in the U.S. Embassy as a guest of Ambassador Herrick. Every day he was feted at luncheons, dinners, and ceremonies. In the capitals of Belgium and England, he was welcomed by thousands.

About a week later, President Calvin Coolidge ordered a navy flagship, the cruiser U.S.S. *Memphis*, to bring Charles A. Lindbergh and the *Spirit of St. Louis* back to the United States for a hero's homecoming.

6

Ambassador by Air

On the morning of June 11, 1927, the *Memphis* arrived at the Washington Navy Yard dock, and a gangplank was hoisted to her rail. While cannons boomed a salute and planes roared overhead, Vice Admiral Guy H. Burrage, commander of the *Memphis*, escorted Evangeline Lindbergh aboard. President Coolidge had arranged for Lindbergh's mother to be the first to greet him.

After a private reunion, the Lindberghs were greeted by members of the Cabinet and other dignitaries. Riding in an open car, they joined the parade of cars, motorcycles, and cavalry. Along the streets of Washington, they were saluted with shouts, cheers, and tears of joy by the admiring crowd—the largest in Washington's history.[1]

At the Washington Monument, the lawn was packed with spectators. Band music filled the air, and thousands applauded as President and Mrs. Coolidge welcomed the young American hero and his mother to the festive reviewing stand.

In his speech before the crowd, President Coolidge praised Lindbergh's achievement. He then pinned the Distinguished Flying Cross, the first ever issued, on the hero's lapel, "as a symbol of appreciation for what he is and what he has done." The president also announced the promotion of Charles A. Lindbergh to colonel in the Army Air Service Reserve Corps.[2]

In response, Lindbergh told of his recent days in Europe and read the message he was asked to bring back. "You have seen the affection of the people of France for the people of America demonstrated to you. When you return to America take back that message to the people of the United States from the people of France and of Europe."[3]

That evening, Lindbergh was the guest of honor at a meeting of the National Press Club in the Washington Auditorium. Six thousand people attended. Speaker Richard V. Oulahan referred to Lindbergh as a young "Ambassador of Good Will," personifying to Europe the real spirit of America.[4]

At a breakfast meeting on Monday, June 13, Lindbergh received a lifetime membership in the National Aeronautic Association. Then he left from Washington's Bolling Field for New York City, where he was to be honored with a ticker-tape parade the next day.

Perched on top of the rear seat of a touring car, Lindbergh and a silk-hatted Mayor James Walker were showered with ticker tape and confetti as they rode up Broadway to City Hall. There, Lindbergh was awarded the Medal of Valor. The parade continued to Central Park, where Governor Alfred E. Smith presented Lindbergh with the New York State Medal of Honor. An estimated four million people lined the streets of New York City that day.[5]

On June 16, Raymond Orteig presented Lindbergh with a check for $25,000 and pronounced him the official winner of the Orteig Prize.[6]

As Charles Lindbergh rode up Broadway in triumph, millions of New Yorkers cheered his historic flight.

Lindbergh's financial backers and others in St. Louis had been waiting for his return to their city. On Friday morning, June 17, Lindbergh took off in the *Spirit of St. Louis* for his home in St. Louis. Landing at Lambert Field, he had to be protected by soldiers from the overenthusiastic crowd. The next day he rode in a triumphal seven-mile parade, where thousands turned out to welcome the hero they claimed as their own.[7] On Sunday, Lindbergh gave an acrobatic flying exhibition over Forest Park and attended a round of affairs in his honor.

Next, Lindbergh flew to Dayton, Ohio, to spend the night as a guest of Orville Wright, the surviving airplane inventor. "It was a sincere gesture, and Orville Wright never forgot it," wrote Marvin W. McFarland, editor of *The Papers of Wilbur and Orville Wright.*[8]

Earlier, Lindbergh had signed a contract with publisher G. P. Putnam's Sons to write a book about his Paris flight. Putnam's wanted the book brought out as soon as possible, so the writing needed to begin immediately.[9]

Harry Guggenheim and his wife, Carol, offered Lindbergh the use of a bedroom suite on their estate, Falaise, in which to write. The twenty-six-room manor house was located on Sands Point, Long Island, New York. There, away from all the newsmen and hero-worshiping crowds, he wrote most of every day.[10]

Lindbergh completed the sixty-thousand-word manuscript in about three weeks. He titled his book "*WE.*" A brief account of his early life and the transatlantic flight, the book sold 190,000 copies in less than eight weeks.[11]

By then, Lindbergh's opportunities to endorse products, or accept high-paying promotional jobs, had reached a total of $5 million. He turned down most of the offers. Lindbergh would endorse only the products he used—such as the Vacuum oil and Champion spark plugs he put in his plane and the Waterman fountain pen with which he wrote in his flight log.[12]

At that time, Charles Lindbergh's major interest was in helping to develop commercial aviation. When the Daniel Guggenheim Fund for the Promotion of Aeronautics suggested that Lindbergh do a forty-eight-state tour in the *Spirit of St. Louis,* he willingly accepted. He would be paid $50,000.[13]

The tour was set up with cooperation from the U.S. Department of Commerce, which would supply another plane, carrying a department aide, Donald E. Keyhoe, hired to manage the tour, along with two assistants.

The route went north from New York City, west to Seattle, and back east from San Diego to Pennsylvania. On July 20, 1927, Lindbergh took off from Mitchell Field, New York. He would be making overnight stops in each of the forty-eight states.

Wherever Lindbergh landed, throngs jammed into the area to see their hero. They cheered his presence, but many barely listened to his words about aviation. Everywhere, Lindbergh was asked about his personal life—about girls, his mother, his hobbies. When he sent shirts to the laundry, people kept them as souvenirs. Admirers wrote him letters, sent gifts, touched him, pushed him, and once tried to yank him out of a parade car.[14]

Along the way, some incidents were of personal satisfaction to Lindbergh. In Grand Rapids, Michigan, he took his mother on a short flight; at Ford Airport in Detroit, Lindbergh talked automaker Henry Ford into taking his first airplane ride; in Little Falls, Minnesota, businesses closed for the day, and

Throngs of people crowded Forest Park in St. Louis, Missouri, to celebrate their local hero, Charles Lindbergh.

thousands of people waited in a pasture north of town for their local hero to arrive.[15]

The tour ended in Philadelphia on October 22, 1927, after 22,350 miles, with stops in eighty-two cities. It accomplished what Lindbergh had set out to do—making the country aware that aviation was a safe way to travel, gaining support for building more airfields, and improving the existing ones.[16]

Upon Lindbergh's return, Dwight W. Morrow, ambassador to Mexico, invited Lindbergh to fly the *Spirit of St. Louis* to Mexico City as a gesture of friendship by the United States. They agreed on a date and time for the *Spirit* to arrive. Lindbergh planned that after the visit, he would fly on to South America. This would be a step toward linking the two Western Hemisphere continents by air.[17]

The morning of December 13, Lindbergh took off from Washington, D.C., for his 2,100-mile flight to Mexico City. Flying through rain, mist, and fog slowed his progress. After twenty-seven hours and fifteen minutes in the air, Lindbergh landed at Valbuena Field in Mexico City. He was two hours late.

Thousands of people had been waiting at the airport. "I was terribly embarrassed," Lindbergh wrote later, "but President Plutarco Calles greeted me warmly as though my wheels had touched the ground on time."[18]

Lindbergh was a guest of Ambassador and Mrs. Morrow at the U.S. Embassy, and his arrival in Mexico stirred up a full week of celebration. Mexican folk dancing, rodeos staged especially for him, rides through the floating gardens—all created a feeling of joy and friendship.

Ambassador Morrow was lauded by the American press for establishing unusually cordial relations with Mexico. President Calles hailed Lindbergh's visit as the beginning of "closer spiritual and material relations" between the United States and Mexico.[19]

Meanwhile, Charles Lindbergh was getting acquainted with the younger members of the Morrow family—their son, Dwight Jr., and daughters, outgoing Elisabeth, who was the oldest; quiet, petite Anne, a senior at Smith College; and spirited fourteen-year-old Constance. He found them easy to talk with, and they were especially curious about flying.

Ambassador and Mrs. Morrow had invited Mrs. Lindbergh to spend Christmas at the embassy, and Henry Ford arranged for her to be flown to Mexico in a new Ford trimotor. This large plane gave Lindbergh the opportunity to take the entire Morrow family on their first flight. Afterward, the young Morrows talked about this new experience. Anne, who was usually shy, spoke eagerly about "how glorious it was—the soaring lift, really the way you dream of it." Lindbergh grinned and nodded.[20]

On December 28, Mrs. Lindbergh was flown back to Detroit, and Lindbergh took off in the *Spirit* on his goodwill flight south. His first stop was Guatemela City. He landed in the capital city of each Central American country and in the Canal Zone. He flew to Colombia, Venezuela, and the Caribbean countries. From Havana, Cuba, Lindbergh flew to St. Louis. Schools closed at noon that day so that sixty thousand children, each with an American flag, could welcome him.[21]

Lindbergh had flown 9,390 miles. In all sixteen countries that he visited, he demonstrated the capability of the airplane and created a feeling of goodwill for the United States.[22]

At the end of 1927, *Time* magazine named Charles A. Lindbergh its "Man of the Year." He was the first person to be so honored. At a White House ceremony in March 1928, Lindbergh was awarded the Congressional Medal of Honor.

On April 30, 1928, Lindbergh presented the *Spirit of St. Louis* to the Smithsonian Institution in Washington, D.C. It remains there on permanent display in the National Air and Space Museum.[23]

At the time, Lindbergh revealed to a few close associates that this would be his last gesture as a professional hero. He was retiring to a private life. From then on, he simply wanted to be a young pilot, and he would not talk to reporters unless he had a comment about aeronautics.[24]

The Pilot and His Mate

Lindbergh began his new career in the aviation business in May 1928. He accepted work as technical consultant for two separate airlines—Transcontinental Air Transport (TAT), and Pan American Airways (Pan Am).

TAT (later, Trans World Airlines, or TWA) was planning passenger service from New York to California by linking airplanes and railroads. Lindbergh's work was to lay out the shortest route from coast to coast for trains and airplanes to connect with each other. When finished, the entire coast-to-coast trip would take forty-eight hours.[1]

As a consultant for Pan Am, Lindbergh's work took him to Central and South America. He surveyed the areas for new air routes, located possible landing fields, and advised about the type of aircraft to use. For him, this work was a way of pursuing a cause to which he was devoted—he wanted to see an end to prejudices between nations and use aviation as a means of creating links.[2]

Now that Charles Lindbergh was twenty-six years old and established in an aviation career, his thoughts turned to a personal matter. "I had always taken for granted that someday I would marry and have a family of my own," he wrote in his autobiography.[3]

One of his requirements was that he wanted "to marry a girl who liked flying." He would take her with him on the expeditions he expected to make in his plane. "That ought to be great fun," he wrote.[4]

Lindbergh decided that he would like to see again one of Ambassador Morrow's daughters. He was thinking of Anne—blue-eyed, dark-haired, extremely pretty—who seemed overshadowed by her vivacious older sister, Elisabeth.

Anne Spencer Morrow, twenty-two years old, had recently graduated from Smith College. Known for her literary talent, she had won two major prizes for essays and poetry.

In October 1928, Lindbergh phoned Anne Morrow at her family home in Englewood, New Jersey, and asked if she would care to go on a flight over Long Island Sound. Taken by surprise, Anne Morrow said, "I–I'd love to."[5] They made a date for the following week.

Anne Morrow's surprise was genuine. She had been thinking of Lindbergh a lot. A summer entry from her diary reads: "As for Colonel L. . . . Here is the finest man I have ever met . . . and someone utterly opposite to me. So opposite that I don't exist at all for him."[6]

For his date with Anne Morrow, Lindbergh rented a small, open-cockpit biplane with dual controls. To avoid newsmen and photographers, he arranged with Harry and Carol Guggenheim to use the horse pasture on their estate for takeoff and landing. He handed Anne a helmet and goggles and explained about the parachute. He also explained about the stick and rudder. While airborne, he briefly allowed her to take over the controls. The flight went well.

Their next date involved a lengthy drive on New Jersey roads in Lindbergh's Franklin sedan. Soon after, they became engaged. In November, they met at the embassy in Mexico City to share their news with Ambassador and Mrs. Morrow. Anne's father insisted that they be formally engaged and get to know each other better. Her mother was surprised but rose to the occasion. "Anne, you'll have the sky," she said.[7]

On February 12, 1929, Ambassador Morrow announced the engagement of Anne Spencer Morrow to Colonel Charles A. Lindbergh. At once, they became a headline couple. Reporters followed them everywhere. To avoid being harassed, they had to stop doing ordinary things—shopping, going to movies, dining in restaurants, or just taking walks. The only place offering freedom from the press and the curious public was in an airplane. They often took secret flights together from the Guggenheim estate.

On May 27, 1929, Anne Morrow became Mrs. Charles Lindbergh. They were married in the large

Charles and Anne Lindbergh a few weeks after their marriage in 1929.

parlor of Next Day Hill, the Morrows' new home in Englewood, New Jersey. Dr. William Adams Brown of Union Theological Seminary performed the wedding ceremony. To ensure privacy from the press, a small group of family and close friends had been invited by phone for an afternoon of lunch and bridge. The guests did not know that they would be witnessing a marriage ceremony.[8]

Afterward, the bride and groom huddled down in the back seat of a car driven by a friend, and slipped past the reporters gathered outside the gate. From a point on the Long Island shore, they boarded a thirty-eight-foot cabin boat for a honeymoon cruise along the New England coastline.

Two days later, they were spotted from the air, then pursued in a speedboat by reporters and cameramen. While the newlyweds remained inside their cabin, the speedboat buzzed around their cruiser for eight hours before leaving. So ended the Lindberghs' honeymoon.

Anne Lindbergh plunged eagerly into her husband's world of aviation. Together, in an open-cockpit biplane, they flew across the country on passenger route surveys for TAT. They flew across Central and South America, and the Caribbean on airmail route surveys for Pan Am.

In the fall of 1929, Lindbergh began planning a Pan Am survey flight from New York to China. He ordered a custom-designed monoplane to be built by the Lockheed Aircraft Corporation in San Diego, California. The couple spent the winter on the West Coast, where Lindbergh could supervise the plane's construction.

Charles and Anne Lindbergh stand beside the Sirius, *in which they will travel to China.*

While there, Anne Lindbergh studied navigation and learned how to find the exact position of their plane during flight. She also learned glider flying and became the first woman in the United States to obtain a glider pilot's license.[9]

In the spring of 1930, the Lindberghs' new plane, with a top speed of 185 MPH, was finished. The dual-control, single-wing plane had two seats, one in front of the other. A sliding transparent cover could be pulled over the seats to make a closed cockpit. They named the plane *Sirius* after the brightest star in the sky.[10]

On Easter Sunday, April 20, 1930, with his wife as navigator, Charles Lindbergh flew the *Sirius* from Los Angeles to New York in fourteen hours and forty-five minutes. With one stop for refueling, their flight set a new transcontinental speed record.

On June 22, 1930, Charles Augustus Lindbergh, Jr., was born at Next Day Hill in Englewood. It was his mother's twenty-fourth birthday.[11]

The following month, Anne Lindbergh's older sister, Elisabeth, had a heart attack, due to a damaged heart valve. Charles Lindbergh consulted with Dr. Alexis Carrel, Nobel Prize winner in medicine, and was told that repair was not possible. No method had been developed to keep organs alive outside the body during surgery.[12] Lindbergh expressed an interest in experimenting to create such a device, and Dr. Carrel offered to share his laboratory at the Rockefeller Institute for Medical Research. Lindbergh began to work on the project whenever possible.

The Lindberghs had never had a home of their own. When not flying, they stayed at the spacious

Morrow estate in Englewood. In the summer of 1930, Charles Lindbergh bought 425 acres of woodland in the Sourland Mountains, near Hopewell, New Jersey. He ordered one-quarter of the land to be cleared for a landing field, and he hired an architect to draw plans for their future home.

Meanwhile, they rented a small New Jersey farm-house about a two-hour drive from Lindbergh's New York office. With a hired couple, Elsie and Oliver Whateley, as housekeepers, and a nurse, Betty Gow, to care for the baby, the Lindberghs began preparing for the China flight.

Both Charles and Anne Lindbergh needed a license to operate the radio in the *Sirius.* This meant passing an examination to send Morse code (a system of dots and dashes that represent letters) at fifteen words a minute. No long-distance voice radio was available at that time. After studying with a private instructor, they passed the examination.

Charles Lindbergh had taught his wife to fly, but as copilot on the China trip, she would need to qual-ify for a pilot's license. In May 1931, he gave her a series of lessons at the Aviation Country Club in Hicksville, Long Island. On May 29, Anne Lindbergh received a transport pilot's license—the highest-grade flying license possible to obtain.[13]

The *Sirius* carried enough gasoline to travel two thousand miles, and Lindbergh arranged for refueling along the way. The plane had been equipped with pontoons, enabling it to land on lakes in northern Canada and along coastlines of the Bering Sea and beyond. A small generator in the plane allowed the

Lindberghs to wear electrically heated flying suits. Other clothing was limited to eighteen pounds each, including the suitcase.

During their absence, one-year-old Charles Jr. would be in the care of his nurse, Betty Gow, and his grandparents, Elizabeth and Dwight Morrow. They would spend the summer at the Morrows' island home on Deacon's Point in North Haven, Maine.

On July 27, 1931, the Lindberghs took off in the *Sirius* from Flushing Bay at College Point, Long Island, and flew to North Haven for the night. Here, while sharing their travel plans with the family, Anne Lindbergh tucked her son into bed one last time before leaving. The next morning, Anne and Charles Lindbergh climbed aboard the *Sirius* and began their pioneer flight.

The first overnight stop was Ottawa, Canada. They met aviators, explorers, and others who knew much about northern Canada. The experts told Lindbergh his planned route was too dangerous. One man announced that he would not take *his* wife over the rugged Canadian wilderness. Lindbergh looked at his wife with a smile, "You must remember," he replied, "*she* is *crew*."[14]

They took off the next morning, using Lindbergh's planned route. Yes, Anne Lindbergh was "crew"—copilot, radio operator, navigator. She also kept a journal of their ten-thousand-mile flight.

The Lindberghs flew the great circle route: to Point Barrow, Alaska; across the Bering Sea to the Kamchatka Peninsula in the Soviet Union; south along the mountainous, fog-shrouded coast; and over the Kuril Islands to Japan. At the harbor city of Nemuro, and again in Tokyo, they were greeted by smiling crowds. *"Banzai! Banzai!"* the Japanese fans shouted. *(Banzai* means "May you live ten thousand years!")[15]

After a two-month journey, the Lindberghs arrived in China. Landing at Nanjing, they learned that millions of people were homeless and starving after the Yangtze River flood. At once, they assisted in relief work, flying food and medicine to isolated areas. At Hankow, the British airplane carrier H.M.S. *Hermes* served as their temporary home, even hoisting the *Sirius* up from flood water that moved too swiftly for a safe mooring of the plane on its pontoons.

Charles and Anne landed the Sirius *on the flooded Yangtze River in Nanking, China.*

On the final day of their emergency work, the *Sirius* overturned while being lowered into the treacherous current. Already in the plane, the Lindberghs had to jump into the river to avoid being trapped under a wing. As they struggled in the muddy Yangtze, sailors in a lifeboat came to their rescue. They both recovered, but the *Sirius* was damaged.

On October 6, while aboard the *Hermes*, Anne Lindbergh received a cable from her sister Elisabeth. Their father had died in his sleep from a stroke.

Immediately, the Lindberghs made plans to return home. They shipped their plane to the Lockheed Aircraft factory in California for repair, and booked passage on an ocean liner for a return trip to the United States.

Tragedy at Home

The Lindberghs arrived at the Morrow home, Next Day Hill, in Englewood on October 23. Dwight Morrow's funeral had taken place earlier. Now they hoped to be of some comfort to Anne Lindbergh's widowed mother. Also, they were pleased to return to their young son.

"He is a strong independent boy," Anne Lindbergh wrote to her mother-in-law, "swaggering around on his firm little legs."[1] Charles Jr. was a healthy, blond, bright child—perfectly normal except for two slightly overlapping toes.[2]

Early in 1932, the Lindberghs began moving into their not-quite-finished new home near Hopewell, New Jersey. The whitewashed stone house had ten rooms, with a separate wing for their live-in cook and housekeeper.

Charles Augustus Lindbergh, Jr., on his first birthday, June 22, 1931.

During the week, they lived in Englewood, an easy drive to Lindbergh's New York City office. On Saturdays, they drove to Hopewell, returning to Englewood on Monday mornings.

On Monday, February 29, Charles Jr. had a severe cold. His mother decided to keep him indoors and not return to Englewood. On Tuesday, March 1, Betty Gow arrived to help out. Meanwhile, Charles Lindbergh called from his office saying he had been delayed and would be late for dinner.

That evening, Anne Lindbergh and Betty Gow prepared Charles Jr. for bed. They tucked him in his crib in the nursery and closed the shutters, except for one that was warped. Charles Lindbergh arrived home later, and after dinner, he and his wife sat and talked in the living room. Once, he heard a cracking sound, but did not investigate. Around ten o'clock, Anne went upstairs to prepare for bed, and Charles settled at his desk in the library. About that time, Betty Gow entered the nursery to check on the baby. His crib was empty.

Quickly, she checked with his mother to see if she had taken him. No, she had not, but maybe his father had him. Betty Gow raced downstairs to the library.

"Colonel, do you have the baby?" she asked anxiously.

"Isn't he in his crib?" Lindbergh responded.

Not waiting for a reply, Lindbergh bounded up the stairs to the nursery. From the appearance of the bedding in the crib, he knew the baby could not have gotten out by himself. Turning to his wife, he said, "Anne, they have stolen our baby."[3]

An envelope was found by a nursery window—the one with the warped shutter. Muddy footprints tracked across the floor. Lindbergh ordered that no one touch anything. He called the local police, the New Jersey State Police, and his lawyer and friend, Henry Breckinridge. The police arrived and checked the envelope for fingerprints. There were none. The kidnapper had worn gloves. Inside, a crudely written, misspelled note demanded a ransom of $50,000, saying: "After 2–4 days we will inform you were to deliver the mony." The note warned not to notify the police, and ended with "The child is in gut [good] care."[4]

Exploring the grounds, police found muddy footprints under the nursery window. Several feet away, they found a wooden ladder with a broken rung. That may have been the cracking sound Lindbergh had heard earlier.

The Lindberghs' only concern was for the safe return of their twenty-month-old child. When reporters and cameramen began arriving, Lindbergh kept the grounds open to them. His three-car garage became temporary police headquarters.

One week later, contact was made by the supposed kidnappers. A retired schoolteacher, John F. Condon, volunteered to serve as a go-between. Through contact with him, the kidnappers produced the sleep suit that Charles Jr. had been wearing on the night of the kidnapping. This convinced the Lindberghs that their child would be delivered the moment they paid the ransom.[5]

Late one night, Condon delivered the $50,000 cash (in marked bills) to a man waiting behind a tombstone in a Bronx cemetery. Lindbergh, waiting in the car, heard the man speak. "Hey, Doctor. Over here!" The voice had a heavy German accent. Lindbergh would never forget that voice.[6]

In exchange for the cash, Condon was given a note, which he delivered to Lindbergh. The note said that the boy was on a boat named Nelly, "between Horsenecks Beach and Gay Head near Elisabeth Island."[7] Lindbergh flew back and forth over the area for the next several days. There was no such boat. Charles Lindbergh had been cruelly tricked. Undaunted, he continued his search, following every reasonable lead.

On the morning of May 12, 1932, the child's body was found in a shallow grave in the woods, a few miles from the Lindbergh home. At the county morgue, Lindbergh identified the body. Carefully examining the teeth and the foot with the slightly overlapping toes, he said, "I'm perfectly satisfied this is my child."[8] The body was cremated that afternoon. Later, Lindbergh would scatter the ashes from his plane, as he had scattered his father's ashes years before.

In reviewing the evidence, investigators on the case concluded that when the rung on the ladder snapped, the kidnapper accidentally dropped the bag containing the child onto the flagstone below. The detectives listed the cause of death as a "fractured skull due to external violence."[9]

Charles and Anne Lindbergh left their Hopewell home, never to spend another night there. They donated the estate to the state of New Jersey for a children's home.[10]

Charles Jr. was stolen from his crib in the new family home near Hopewell, New Jersey. After their son was found dead, the Lindberghs knew they could no longer live in this house.

The search for the kidnapper continued, with the police investigating every rumor. The Lindberghs moved back to Next Day Hill, into a wing of the house. Although a security system was in place and state troopers patrolled the grounds, kidnap threats prompted Lindbergh to purchase a guard dog. He trained the enormous German shepherd, Thor, to be obedient and fiercely protective of his owners.[11]

On August 16, 1932, Anne Lindbergh gave birth to their second son, Jon. When Lindbergh released a birth announcement to the press, he issued a statement saying that publicity was "in a large measure" responsible for the death of their first child. "I am appealing to the press to permit our children to lead the lives of normal Americans."[12]

In the spring of 1933, Charles Lindbergh began drawing plans for a northern air route to Europe—via Labrador, Greenland, and Iceland to Denmark and other northern European countries. He also began plotting a southern route from the western coast of Africa to South America. The purpose of the trip would be to provide information Pan Am could use to develop passenger service across the Atlantic.

On July 9, 1933, Charles and Anne Lindbergh took off on their North Atlantic flight. Evangeline Lindbergh would care for Jon, her eleven-month-old grandson, at the Morrows' summerhouse in Maine. Armed guards would provide security around the grounds.

Once again the Lindberghs traveled in the *Sirius*, with Anne Lindbergh serving as copilot, navigator, and radio operator. When the *Sirius* anchored in the harbor of Holsteinsborg, Greenland, the residents crowded along the dock excitedly crying out, "Tingmissartoq! Tingmissartoq!" The Inuit word means "the one who flies like a big bird." That word appealed to the Lindberghs. Before leaving, they asked a young Greenlander to paint Tingmissartoq on the fuselage of the *Sirius.* That became its new name.[13]

Their flight lasted more than five months. Leaving Greenland and Iceland, they visited fourteen European countries and two African countries. They returned across the Atlantic Ocean to Brazil, Trinidad, and Puerto Rico. In 1938, Anne Lindbergh would publish an account of the Africa-to-Brazil segment of their journey under the title *Listen! The Wind.*

Arriving in New York in December 1933, the Lindberghs gave the *Tingmissartoq* to the American Museum of Natural History in New York City. Later, the plane was transferred to the Smithsonian Institution in Washington, D.C.[14]

Early in 1934, President Franklin D. Roosevelt believed some aviation companies were receiving airmail contracts even though they had not submitted the lowest bids. On February 9, he issued an order canceling the airmail contracts of all private aviation companies and turning the flying of airmail over to the U.S. Army Air Corps.

Charles Lindbergh protested the cancellation. He warned that the army pilots' lack of training for airmail flying could result in deaths. Tragedy soon occurred. By the end of the first week, five pilots were dead, six were injured, and eight planes were wrecked.[15]

On March 16, Lindbergh testified in a Senate hearing on a bill to return the transporting of airmail to private aviation companies. Two months after the bill passed, commercial airlines once again carried airmail.[16]

On September 28, 1934, Bruno Richard Hauptmann was arrested by the police as a suspect in the kidnap-murder of Charles A. Lindbergh, Jr. A gas station attendant had recognized one of the marked ransom bills he received for payment of gas. He jotted down the car's license number and reported it to the police.

Investigating the Bronx home of Hauptmann, police and FBI agents found $14,000 of the ransom money nailed behind some boards in the garage. Later, experts matched the wood from a ladder found in Hauptmann's house to the wood from the ladder used in the kidnapping.[17]

Other evidence was gathered, including Lindbergh's recognition of Hauptmann's voice as the one he heard at the cemetery. In October 1934, following a grand jury hearing in the county courthouse in Flemington, New Jersey, Hauptmann was charged with murder in the first degree.[18]

The trial began on January 2, 1935, in Flemington. Hundreds of reporters and photographers arrived to cover the story. Judge Thomas W. Trenchard of Trenton, New Jersey, presided over the trial, which lasted almost six weeks. Lindbergh came every day to watch the proceedings, and several times he was called to the witness stand. Anne Lindbergh appeared in the courtroom only once, when she was needed to testify.

On February 13, 1935, the jury found Hauptmann guilty of murder in the first degree. Judge Trenchard sentenced him to death, with an execution date set for March 1935.[19]

For the Lindberghs, a secure life continued to be a struggle. The verdict brought many threatening letters. One afternoon when Betty Gow was driving Jon home from nursery school, a black car forced them to a sudden stop against the curb. Terrified, she thought gangsters were stopping them.

A photographer jumped out, rushed to the rear car window, and repeatedly took flashbulb photos of the frightened, crying child.[20] Then he drove away.

Although it had only been a tabloid photographer, there were enough kidnap threats, fanatics, and news reporters to make everyday living uncomfortable. Lindbergh decided to move his family to a place where they might gain more security and peace.

On Saturday, December 21, 1935, late at night, the three Lindberghs quietly boarded the freighter *American Importer* and sailed for England.[21]

Sunshine and Shadows

Early in 1936, the Lindberghs moved into Long Barn, a country home in Kent, England. They rented the rambling barn and cottage from Harold Nicolson, a member of Parliament, and his wife, the novelist Vita Sackville-West. Nicolson had written a biography of Anne's father, the late Dwight Morrow.

When the Lindberghs first arrived in England, their presence stirred the curiosity of British reporters, but interest soon faded. At Long Barn the vast garden provided privacy. Jon played outdoors without a guard, and his mother began writing a book about the North Atlantic survey flight. Anne Morrow Lindbergh's first book, *North to the Orient,* had been published in August 1935 and became an immediate best-seller in the United States.[1]

Charles Lindbergh hired a secretary and worked on correspondence. He stayed in close communication with friends who were working on projects of special interest to him: Robert H. Goddard, Harry Guggenheim, and Dr. Alexis Carrel.

Robert Goddard, a science professor at Clark University in Worcester, Massachusetts, shared Lindbergh's vision of rocketry as a way of future flight. Goddard believed that a rocket could be developed that might even reach the moon. Lindbergh persuaded Harry Guggenheim to provide an initial grant of $50,000 for Goddard to build an experimental rocket station near Roswell, New Mexico. Here Goddard could work full-time on developing higher-soaring rockets. His pioneering research would open the way to the Space Age.[2]

Lindbergh's work with Dr. Alexis Carrel on developing a means of keeping organs alive outside the body during heart surgery was ongoing. In June 1935, their coauthored article in *Science* magazine had announced the development of a perfusion pump. The thyroid gland of a cat, when placed in the pump, lived for 120 days. A major breakthrough for surgical medicine, the perfusion pump was referred to as an "artificial heart" by some newspapers.[3] At Long Barn, Lindbergh set up a small laboratory in which to do further research. Though separated by distance, both men continued with their scientific study.

Back in New Jersey, Bruno Richard Hauptmann maintained his innocence. Throughout the past year, his attorneys had filed several appeals delaying his execution. When no evidence of his innocence could be found, Hauptmann was executed in the state prison on April 3, 1936. The reaction of the Lindberghs to this event was never publicly revealed.[4]

In the spring, Lindbergh received a letter from Major Truman Smith, the United States military attaché in Berlin, Germany. It was an invitation, in the name of General Hermann Goering and the German Air Ministry, "to visit Germany and inspect the new German civil and military air establishments." Major Smith added that from an American point of view, "your visit here would be of high patriotic benefit."[5]

Major Smith's chief duty was to report to the General Staff in Washington, D.C., about the growth of the German army. Lindbergh's assessment on the size and strength of the Luftwaffe (German air force) would be helpful.[6]

On July 22, 1936, Charles and Anne Lindbergh flew to Berlin in their Mohawk monoplane, built in England. They would stay with Major Smith and his wife, Kay Smith.

Although the United States was uneasy about Germany at the time, both governments were still on fairly good terms. Because the United States' own military attaché had urged Lindbergh to come to Germany, the visit was accepted without criticism.[7]

Lindbergh received a hero's welcome from U.S. military personnel and German aviation officials. As guest of honor, he spoke at an Air Club of Berlin luncheon. "Aviation has brought a revolutionary change to a world already staggering from changes," Lindbergh said. Then he cautioned, "It is our responsibility to make sure that in doing so, we do not destroy the very things which we wish to protect."[8]

Lindbergh was taken on inspection tours of airports, airplane factories, and an air research institute. He saw the latest dive-bomber, fighter, and observation planes. He piloted a Luftwaffe bombardment plane. After observing the efficiency of the German system, Lindbergh noted that Germany could manufacture military aircraft faster than any other country in Europe, perhaps even faster than the United States.[9]

In London, on May 12, 1937, the Lindberghs' third son was born. They named him Land, after Evangeline Land Lindbergh's side of the family.

A second trip to Germany was made in October, and Lindbergh attended the Lilienthal Aeronautical Society Congress. Again, he was permitted to inspect German aircraft.

In November 1937, Lindbergh helped Major Truman Smith prepare an intelligence report stressing the strength of the Luftwaffe and predicting that its military technology would soon be equal to that of the United States. In Washington, the U.S. General Staff and the Army Air Corps took the report more seriously than the politicians, who believed that Germany was a weak and divided country.[10]

In the spring of 1938, the Lindberghs moved to Illiec, a small island off the coast of France. A nearby island, Saint-Gildas, was the summer home of Dr. Carrel and his wife. On Illiec, Lindbergh set up a laboratory in the barn for Carrel and himself to work on their medical research. *The Culture of Organs*, a book in which they summarized their experiments about the perfusion of organs (keeping organs alive outside the body) was published later that year.[11]

At the request of Major Smith and U.S. ambassador Hugh R. Wilson, the Lindberghs made a third trip to Germany in October 1938. Lindbergh attended a men-only dinner at the American Embassy, where Field Marshall Goering was also a guest. Unexpectedly, he approached Lindbergh, spoke briefly in German, and gave him a small red box. Because Lindbergh did not understand German, the speech was translated. To everyone's surprise, Goering had "in the name of the führer [Adolf Hitler]" awarded Charles Lindbergh the Service Cross of the German Eagle, a high civilian medal. Goering had said the decoration was for Lindbergh's services to aviation and particularly for his 1927 solo flight across the Atlantic.[12]

In late October, the Lindberghs moved into a rented apartment in Paris. On the night of November 9, 1938, the Nazis attacked Jewish businesses and synagogues in Berlin and throughout Germany. The attack became known as *Kristallnacht* (meaning Crystal Night, or the Night of Broken Glass) in reference to the many store windows that were broken. Many Americans were appalled at this Nazi assault on the German Jews.

Occurring only three weeks after Lindbergh had been presented with the German medal, First Lady Eleanor Roosevelt said in dismay, "How could Lindbergh take that Hitler decoration!"[13] As a protest against the anti-Jewish riots, President Roosevelt immediately recalled Ambassador Wilson from Germany. Anne Lindbergh, too, was shocked, calling the attack "stupid and brutal and undisciplined."[14]

Deeply concerned that the United States might be drawn into the impending European conflict, Lindbergh sailed home to the United States in April 1939. After meeting in Washington, D.C., with General Henry H. Arnold, chief of the U.S. Army Air Corps, Lindbergh, a reserve officer in the Army Air Corps, agreed to help the United States decide how to build up its strength in the air.[15] He then cabled his wife in Paris to return with the children on the next available ship.

General Arnold had assigned Lindbergh to promote airplane production. Traveling from coast to coast in an Air Corps fighter plane, he toured laboratories and defense plants, advising on technical design and improvements to facilities. Meanwhile, Anne Lindbergh found a place for the family to live in Lloyd Neck, on the north shore of Long Island.

When the German army advanced into Poland on September 3, 1939, both Britain and France declared war on Germany. President Roosevelt spoke on the radio that night, assuring the American people that he would do everything in his power to keep the United States neutral.

Uneasy about Roosevelt's speech, Lindbergh wrote two radio speeches and an article expressing his feeling about the war in Europe. In his journal he wrote, "I do not intend to stand by and see this country pushed into war, if it is not absolutely essential to the welfare of the nation."[16]

In September, Lindbergh spoke over three major radio networks, urging that the United States stay out of the European conflict. His article "Aviation, Geography and Race" was published in the November 1939 issue of the *Reader's Digest*. Many readers were disturbed by its racist theories.[17]

He wrote of the superiority of the white race ("the heirs of European culture"). Western nations must stick together, he believed: "It is time to turn from our quarrels and to build our White ramparts again. . . . Our civilization depends on a united strength among ourselves." Lindbergh warned against "the infiltration of inferior blood" and "attack by foreign armies and dilution by foreign races."[18]

In support of her husband, Anne Lindbergh wrote a small book urging Americans not to enter the conflict in Europe. *The Wave of the Future* was published in October 1940. The reviews were mostly unfavorable. The book was criticized for suggesting that Nazism, Fascism, and Communism had to be accepted because they were the wave of the future.[19]

After visiting Hitler and Nazi Germany, Charles Lindbergh said that "Hitler must have far more character and vision than I thought existed in the German leader. . . he is undoubtedly a great man, and I believe has done much for the German people."[20] Anne Lindbergh described Hitler as being "like an inspired religious leader—and as such rather fanatical—but... not greedy for power, but a mystic, a visionary who really wants the best for his country."[21]

A fourth child was born to the Lindberghs on October 2, 1940. After three sons, they were

"I do not intend to stand by and see this country pushed into war": Lindbergh spoke out against U.S. involvement in the war in Europe in 1939.

delighted to have a daughter. They named her Anne, after her mother.[22]

By the fall of 1940, the Nazi German Army had invaded and occupied most of western Europe, including France. England struggled alone against bombing attacks from German war planes. The British prime minister, Winston Churchill, appealed to the United States for aid.

President Roosevelt proposed the Lend-Lease Bill to provide Britain with vital war supplies. Lindbergh testified before Congress against the bill. He argued that aid to Great Britain would carry the United States into the war. Despite his opposition and that of others, Congress passed the Lend-Lease Bill, which President Roosevelt signed into law on March 11, 1941.[23]

Some of Charles and Anne Lindbergh's closest friends, who supported aid to Britain, began to distance themselves from Lindbergh: Henry Breckinridge, his longtime lawyer; Harry Guggenheim, who had financed his goodwill tour in 1927; and even Lindbergh's mother-in-law, Elizabeth Morrow, who was active in several organizations providing aid to Britain.[24]

In April 1941, Lindbergh joined the America First Committee—the most powerful isolationist group in the United States. Isolationists were opposed to the United States entry into the European conflict. Lindbergh became the committee's most popular and controversial speaker.[25]

President Roosevelt did not agree with Lindbergh's political views, and he was concerned about Lindbergh's ability to sway others to his beliefs. At a White House press conference on April 25, 1941, the president was asked his opinion of Lindbergh's isolationist views. Why was Colonel Lindbergh, a reserve officer, not being sent to Europe as a pilot? In reply, the president said throughout history there were always people who disagreed with the nation's actions. He compared Lindbergh to the Civil War "Copperheads." Named for a poisonous snake, Yankees who made anti-war speeches were known as Copperheads. In other words, they were considered traitors.[26]

Offended and angry, Lindbergh wrote a letter to the president, resigning his commission as colonel in the Army Air Corps Reserve.[27]

At the America First rally on September 11 in Des Moines, Iowa, Lindbergh spoke to an overflow crowd. He named the groups that he believed were trying to lead the United States into war: "the British, the Jewish, and the Roosevelt administration."[28] He did not want the United States to join the Allied Forces against Nazi Germany.

Lindbergh's speech was highly criticized as anti-Semitic (anti-Jewish). The America First Committee denied that Colonel Lindbergh or its other members were anti-Semitic.[29] Some members of the committee resigned because of this speech. The conservative newspapers owned by William Randolph Hearst had strongly supported Lindbergh. Now they commented: "Charles A. Lindbergh's . . . intolerant address in Des Moines, in which racial and religious prejudices were incited—especially against those of the Jewish faith—should arouse universal protest."[30]

On the morning of December 7, 1941, Japan attacked Pearl Harbor—the United States naval base in Hawaii. The following day, the United States declared war on Japan, entering World War II.

Lindbergh knew he must stand with his country in this crisis. In a press release for the America First Committee, he wrote, "Now [war] has come, and we must meet it as united Americans regardless of our attitude in the past. . . our country has been attacked . . . and we must retaliate. . . . We must now turn every effort to building the greatest and most efficient Army, Navy, and Air Force in the world."[31]

America at War

Three days after the United States declared war on Japan, both Germany and Italy declared war on the United States, in support of Japan. The United States was now at war on two fronts. The entire country began rallying to support the war effort.

In late December, Charles Lindbergh wrote to General Harold Arnold, volunteering his services in the Army Air Corps. General Arnold wanted to accept his offer, but President Roosevelt denied Lindbergh the opportunity because of his prewar isolationist views.[1]

Lindbergh then offered his services as a technical consultant to various aircraft corporations. They, too, were unable to obtain clearance from the government.

Finally, in the spring of 1942, Henry Ford approached Lindbergh about working as a consultant in Ford's Willow Run plant. The Ford Motor Company was now producing four-engine B-24 bombers for the War Department. A work agreement was reached, and this time the government did not object.

Lindbergh had no experience with heavy bombers, but his technical experience proved valuable in working on problems of design, production, and testing.[2]

Lindbergh rented a large house in Bloomfield Hills, near Detroit, where his wife and children joined him. He was pleased to be settled with his family in a home away from the New York press, and near his mother who was now in the early stage of Parkinson's disease.[3]

On August 13, 1942, Anne Lindbergh gave birth to their fifth child—a boy—whom they named Scott.

Although working at Ford, Lindbergh hoped eventually to get into combat action. At a local airfield, he earned a license to fly multiengine planes. Then he joined a Willow Run group of test pilots at the Mayo Clinic's Aeromedical Laboratory. There, in an altitude chamber, he went through numerous oxygen tests to record his mental and physical reactions as the air was steadily thinned. These tests led to improved equipment for emergency parachute jumps at altitudes of thirty-five thousand feet or higher. Lindbergh designed a system in which pulling the parachute rip cord automatically turned on the oxygen jump bottle. This started an immediate flow of needed oxygen to the pilot's mask.[4]

In 1943, Lindbergh also worked for the United Aircraft Corporation in Hartford, Connecticut.

United Aircraft produced Corsair fighter planes for the Navy and the Marine Corps. As technical consultant, he filled such roles as test pilot, instructor, and aeronautical engineer. Demonstrating the Corsair at pilot training centers, he astonished observers with his flying skill. Once, in a high-altitude gunnery contest with two of the best pilots in the Marine Corps, Lindbergh outflew and outshot them both.[5]

In the spring of 1944, United Aircraft sent Lindbergh to the South Pacific as a civilian technical representative. The purpose was to get information helpful in designing future fighter airplanes. He would study fighter planes under combat conditions. He would also instruct U.S. Air Force pilots on how to increase the flying range of the P-38 fighter plane.[6] The P-38 Lightning was a twin-engine plane built by Lockheed Aircraft Corporation. It had a top speed of 410 miles per hour.[7]

Charles Lindbergh was now forty-two years old, almost ancient for a fighter pilot. When a squadron of P-38 pilots on the island of Biak, near New Guinea, heard that Charles Lindbergh was there to show them how to increase their flying range, they reacted with disbelief.

"You mean he's here in the islands?"

They all had heard of his historic flight across the Atlantic. But that was back in 1927.

"How can an old man like him fly with us in a P-38?" asked one of the twenty-year-old flyers.

Lindbergh *did* fly with the squadron, and he *did* demonstrate how different flying techniques could save fuel. As for his flying skill, one of the pilots in

Lindbergh was sent to the South Pacific during World War II. His job was to study fighter planes in action to help the government design better military aircraft.

the squadron, Lieutenant Richard Kirkland, reported later that "the old man" handled the P-38 "like he'd been born in it."[8]

Charles Lindbergh spent almost five months in the South Pacific. He flew fifty combat missions—twenty-five with the Air Force in P-38 Lightnings and twenty-five with the Marine Corps in Corsairs.[9] His combat participation broke military regulations because he was there as a civilian observer. This fact was overlooked, however, by his superior officers. To the military men in aviation, Charles Lindbergh was still a hero. They were happy to support his desire for military action.[10]

On a combat mission on July 28, 1944, Lindbergh experienced a death-defying encounter. Attacked by a Japanese plane, both pilots firing steadily, Lindbergh narrowly missed a head-on crash before shooting down the enemy plane.[11]

General George C. Kenney, commander of Allied Air Forces and the U.S. Fifth Air Force, spoke of Lindbergh's fuel-saving instructions. They extended the flying distance of P-38s by hundreds of miles. "Lindbergh's contribution shortened the war by several months," he said, "and saved thousands of American lives."[12]

During her husband's absence, Anne Lindbergh cared for their children, coped with wartime shortages, attended classes at nearby Cranbrook Academy of Art, and finished working on another book, *The Steep Ascent*. This short novel was based on a frightening experience that occurred when the Lindberghs were trapped in a fogbank over the Alps during their 1937 flight to India.

When she learned that the lease on their Bloomfield Hills house could not be renewed, Anne Lindbergh moved the family to a large house in Westport, Connecticut. Her husband returned from the South Pacific in September 1944, and continued as an adviser with United Aircraft in Hartford, Connecticut.

After Germany surrendered in May 1945, Charles Lindbergh joined a naval technical mission in Europe, as a civilian representative of United Aircraft. The group was sent to Germany, he wrote, "to study the latest development in German aircraft and missiles."[13]

Early in June, the technical mission reached Camp Dora-Mittelbau, a Nazi prison camp near Nordhausen, Germany. It had provided forced labor for a V-2 rocket factory in Nordhausen. A young Polish ex-prisoner took the group on a tour of the prison camp. He showed them two large cremating furnaces used to incinerate twenty-five thousand bodies during the past year and a half. A pit eight feet by six feet overflowed with human ashes and bone fragments.[14]

"Of course, I knew these things were going on," Lindbergh wrote in his journal, "but it is one thing to have the intellectual knowledge, even to look at photographs someone else has taken, and quite another to stand on the scene yourself, seeing, hearing, feeling with your own senses." The experience was deeply disturbing. "It seemed impossible," he wrote, "that men—civilized men—could degenerate to such a level."[15]

Charles Lindbergh continued with United Aircraft until Japan surrendered in August 1945. For the next ten years, he worked actively in military fields: as a member of Chicago Ordnance Research, called CHORE, a top-secret weapons program run by the army at the University of Chicago; as a consultant to the secretary of the air force in Washington; and as a member of the scientific ballistic-missile committee run by the Department of Defense.[16]

Lindbergh assisted in the reorganization of the Strategic Air Command (SAC). He believed that SAC should have enough power to win an atomic war—but more important, it should prevent one. With this goal in mind, he accepted any air force fact-finding assignment. His combined SAC and air force work took him to air force bases around the world.[17]

In 1949, Lindbergh was awarded the Wright Brothers Memorial Trophy by the Aero Club of Washington. In accepting the award, Lindbergh spoke of man's need to "balance science with . . . qualities of body and spirit as well as those of mind." He said the Wright brothers "represented man in balance. And from that balance came wings to lift a world."[18]

From the Institute of the Aeronautical Sciences, in January 1954, Lindbergh received the Daniel Guggenheim Gold Medal for his "pioneering achievement in flight and air navigation."[19]

Also in 1954, President Dwight D. Eisenhower restored Charles A. Lindbergh's military standing. The president made him a brigadier general in the Air Force Reserve Corps.[20]

11

Family and Home

On October 2, 1945, Anne
Lindbergh gave birth to the Lindberghs' sixth and last
child, a daughter whom they named Reeve.

Charles and Anne Lindbergh were now looking for
a permanent family home. In 1946, they bought a
three-story, Tudor-style home on several acres of
property in Darien, Connecticut. Overlooking a
stretch of water flowing into Long Island Sound, the
area was called Scott's Cove. The property had its own
waterfront and was covered with trees and wild growing shrubbery. The stone house had a large living
room with a fireplace, and the various rooms easily
adapted to their casual style of living. Essential were
the many bedrooms and bathrooms, a playroom, two
screened-in porches, a servants' wing, and a home

office for each parent. A trailer parked in the woods gave Anne Lindbergh a secluded place in which to write.[1]

By staying out of the news since 1941, the family had found the feeling of privacy and security they had long wanted. The children attended public schools and often brought school friends home to play. They could shop at the local markets without drawing attention. They were encouraged to be self-reliant, and to share their father's love of nature and outdoor activities.

Charles Lindbergh was a caring but exacting father. "Father" is what the children called him— never "Daddy," as most of their childhood friends addressed their fathers. His towering six-foot-two presence seemed to command formality.

When he was home—that is, when he was not off on a mission for the government or Pan Am—he played games with the children and read to them each night. He taught them to swim, sail, and fish. He also assigned chores and posted a list of rules for everyone to follow. "There were only two ways of doing things," recalled one of the Lindbergh children, "Father's way and the wrong way."[2]

Lindbergh disapproved of candy, unenriched white bread, and comic books. He considered television a bad influence, so the family never owned a television set. Occasionally, one of the children would slip over to a neighbor's house to watch a favorite program.[3]

Charles Lindbergh was protective of his family. As his children approached driving age, he taught each one how to handle a car. They learned not only how to drive but how to check over a vehicle for safety— the tires, brakes, lights, gas, oil, water—and how to handle a car on an icy road.

Lindbergh shared his love of flying with his children by teaching them to fly. On Saturdays, he rented a dual-control plane at the local airport and gave a flying lesson to whoever had reached the right age. Jon learned to fly at sixteen. After twelve hours of instruction, he soloed successfully, and later earned a pilot's license.[4]

While guiding five children through their growing-up years, Charles and Anne Lindbergh also engaged in their own writing projects. In 1948, Charles Lindbergh wrote an essay expressing his thoughts on war and Western civilization. Titled *Of Flight and Life*, this fifty-six-page book, published by Charles Scribner's Sons, sold out on the first day. A second printing sold almost as quickly. John P. Marquand, editorial board member of the Book-of-the-Month Club, praised the book for what Lindbergh had said and for his clarity of thought and literary skill.[5]

Lindbergh had never been satisfied with his hastily written book *"WE,"* about his 1927 New York–Paris flight. For the next twelve years, wherever in the world he happened to be, he wrote down brief recollections of that historic Atlantic crossing. He also wrote down memories of his childhood and of various events from his past. Now he sat in his home office whenever time would allow and worked at arranging his notes into book form. After several rewrites of the manuscript, and with editing help from his author wife, the book became a reality. *The Spirit of St. Louis* was published in 1953. On the dedication page, Lindbergh wrote: "To A.M.L.—Who will never realize how much of this book she has written."[6]

The Spirit of St. Louis became an immediate best-seller, and it was selected by the Book-of-the-Month Club as a main choice. Shortly afterward, the book was bought for filming for a reported $1,000,000. Actor James Stewart was cast to play Charles Lindbergh.[7]

As a book, *The Spirit of St. Louis* received all favorable reviews. In the spring of 1954, Lindbergh was awarded the Pulitzer Prize for biography.[8]

Meanwhile in Detroit, Evangeline Lindbergh had been growing weaker from Parkinson's disease and heart failure. She died in September 1954, at the age of seventy-eight. Three months later, Anne Lindbergh's mother suffered a paralyzing stroke. After a second stroke several weeks later, Elizabeth Cutter Morrow died at the age of eighty-one.[9]

Feeling a sense of loss, and the need for a break from day-to-day family responsibility, Anne Lindbergh rented a four-room cottage on Florida's Captiva Island. Free to bird-watch, collect shells along the beach, and write without interruption, she returned home with the manuscript for a book. Published in 1955, *Gift from the Sea* spoke for a generation of women weary from the demands of their families, their communities, and the pressure to please others. Her book remained on the best-seller list for nearly six months, and she became one of the

Anne and Charles Lindbergh were authors as well as pilots.

most popular and successful writers in the United States.[10]

In 1963, Reeve, the Lindberghs' youngest child, entered college. It was time for the parents to leave their big house. Lindbergh arranged for a smaller house to be built for the two of them at the edge of Scott's Cove. Located several hundred yards from the big house, which they sold, this would now be their permanent home.

Back to Earth

In his years of flying throughout the world, Charles Lindbergh became sharply aware of human destruction of the natural environment. Bulldozers tore down forests for housing developments; cars and trucks polluted the air; factory waste poisoned rivers and lakes. And now, Pan Am was considering buying a supersonic airliner—the Concorde. Flying higher and faster than any other passenger jet, it would carry passengers across the Atlantic in barely more than three hours.[1]

Early in the 1960s, as a director of Pan American Airways, Charles Lindbergh listened to the board meeting discussion and wondered: Did the world really need such a plane? And what might it do to the earth's upper atmosphere? To the dismay of his fellow directors, Lindbergh voted against ordering the Concorde. He believed that the supersonic plane polluted the upper atmosphere and wasted the planet's oil resources, and that its sonic booms were a noisy menace.[2]

Science was developing so fast, it seemed to be a growing threat to both human beings and nature. In 1965, Charles and Anne Lindbergh invited their children and their spouses on a safari to East Africa. They traveled in two Land Rovers, with camping equipment and cameras. They had come to observe and photograph wild animals in their natural world—giraffes, zebras, flocks of gazelle, colonies of baboons, the rhinoceros, and elephants "with white tusks gleaming in the dusk."[3]

When they returned home, Lindbergh's priorities had changed. After a life dedicated to science, he joined the World Wildlife Fund and began to work for conservation and the protection of endangered species.

From then on, he traveled widely to promote awareness of the need to protect both animals and the environment. In Peru, he appealed successfully to ban the harpooning of blue and humpback whales.[4] In Indonesia, he persuaded President Sukarno to offer protection for the Javanese rhinoceros. Lindbergh lobbied with success in the Philippines to preserve the tamarau (a dwarf wild buffalo), and the monkey-eating eagle. He spoke before the legislature in Anchorage, Alaska, for the protection of wolves.[5]

While in the Philippines, Lindbergh learned of a tribe living in caves deep in the rain forest. Known as the Tasaday, they were possibly the last Stone Age

Lindbergh had always loved nature. In his later years he worked to save the environment and protect endangered animals.

culture on earth. After talking with anthropologists who studied the Tasaday, and visiting their tribe, Lindbergh persuaded President Ferdinand E. Marcos to sign a decree creating an area of more than forty-six thousand acres where the Tasadays could live undisturbed.[6]

With many of Lindbergh's World Wildlife Fund activities taking place in the Pacific area, he purchased four acres of forest, cliffs, and seashore on

Maui in the Hawaiian Islands. Here, he built a small vacation cottage. Now, the Lindberghs would spend spring and fall at Scott's Cove, the summer in Switzerland, where Anne had purchased a chalet overlooking Lake Geneva, and the two winter months on Maui—Lindbergh's favorite place.[7]

Lindbergh's enthusiasm for conservation took him all over the world on speaking engagements, and he began to appear more frequently in public on other occasions. In November 1968, both Lindberghs attended the National Institute of Social Sciences annual dinner, where he was awarded a gold medal for "distinguished service to humanity." The following month, President Lyndon Johnson invited them to a White House dinner honoring the Apollo astronauts. Lindbergh spoke to the astronauts about Robert Goddard's belief, forty years earlier, that one day a multistage rocket could reach the moon. Now it was about to come true. At Cape Kennedy, December 21, 1968, the Lindberghs watched the launch of *Apollo 8*, man's first voyage to the moon.[8]

In his mid-sixties, Lindbergh began reading over the journals he had kept between 1938 and 1945. He decided to publish them. In view of the numerous errors in biographies written about him during the war years, he wanted to provide "to the best of my ability, an accurate record."[9]

The Wartime Journals of Charles A. Lindbergh was published in September 1970. It became a best-seller and was a semifinalist for a National Book Award. *Wartime Journals* may not have changed the opinion of readers who opposed his prewar isolationism or who believed he was anti-Semitic. The book did, however, reveal Lindbergh to be a loyal American citizen.[10]

Charles Lindbergh had always encouraged his wife with her writing. He suggested that she publish her diaries beginning with her college years. At first she dreaded the idea, but he persisted.[11] The first volume, *Bring Me a Unicorn*, was published in 1972. In the next five years, she would go on to publish four more volumes.[12]

By the 1970s, the five Lindbergh children were adults with families of their own, and pursuing their careers. Jon graduated from Stanford University with a degree in biology. He trained in the navy as a frogman, and became an oceanographer and deep-sea diver. Land, who like his father was fond of the outdoors, bought a ranch in western Montana and became a successful cattle breeder. Anne, the elder daughter, and Reeve, the younger, both attended Radcliffe College, and both became writers.

Anne wrote short stories and fantasy books for children. Reeve wrote poetry, children's books, and novels. In 1999, Reeve Lindbergh wrote the book *Under a Wing*, a memoir of her famous parents. Scott did graduate work in animal psychology at Strasbourg University in France. He and his wife established an eighty-acre research preserve in the Dordogne area of France, where they study endangered South American primates.[13]

In 1993, the Lindbergh family was saddened by the death of daughter Anne. She died at age fifty-three from melanoma—a type of cancer.[14]

Charles Lindbergh visited his boyhood home in Minnesota in September 1973. He had been invited to speak at the dedication of the Lindbergh Interpretive Center in Little Falls. This small, modern museum displays many historic items relating to the Lindbergh family. During his visit, Lindbergh stood on the steps of the restored farmhouse and spoke on the importance of preserving and improving "the quality of life—all life, not human life alone."[15]

Lindbergh had been diagnosed with lymphoma, a form of cancer, in 1972. After a series of radiation treatments, he spent several months in Maui recuperating. With little improvement, he returned to Scott's Cove in Darien, and resigned from the boards of the World Wildlife Fund and Pan Am.

He entered Columbia-Presbyterian Hospital in New York City for treatment in the summer of 1974, but his condition worsened. When Lindbergh was told there was little hope for recovery, he arranged to be flown to Maui for his final days. Anne Lindbergh, Jon, and Land accompanied him. Although confined to bed, he made his own funeral arrangements, including the hymns to be sung.

Charles Lindbergh died on August 26, 1974. He was seventy-two years old. He was buried in the cemetery beside the Palapala Ho'omau Congregational Church in Kipahulu.[16]

In 1999, *Time* magazine featured Charles A. Lindbergh as one of the "100 Heroes of the 20th

*Lindbergh spent his last days in his favorite place—Maui, Hawaii.
He asked to be buried near this small church.*

Century."[17] A pioneer in aeronautics, and in the
development of an "artificial heart," he was an isolationist who fought for his country in World War II, and
a protector of nature's world. Charles A. Lindbergh
envisioned new possibilities and made them happen.

The lone pilot, once heralded as America's hero,
had become a hero of the twentieth century.

1902—Charles A. Lindbergh is born February 4 in Detroit, Michigan.

1918—Graduates from Little Falls High School, Little Falls, Minnesota.

1920—Attends University of Wisconsin, in Madison.

1922—Leaves college to attend flying school in Lincoln, Nebraska; barnstorms as mechanic, wing-walker, and parachute jumper.

1923—Buys a plane; first solo flight; barnstorms.

1924—Enters Army Air Service training school in San Antonio, Texas; father, C. A. Lindbergh, dies.

1925—Graduates with top honors; becomes a commissioned officer in the Army Air Service Reserve Corps.

1926—As pilot, flies first airmail from St. Louis to Chicago; seeks financing for a nonstop flight to Paris.

1927—Designs the *Spirit of St. Louis;* flies nonstop across Atlantic Ocean from New York to Paris; writes *"WE."*

1928—Is technical consultant to Transcontinental Air Transport and Pan American Airways.

1929—Marries Anne Morrow.

1930—Charles Lindbergh, Jr., is born June 22.

1931—Lindberghs fly from New York to China, surveying for air routes.

1932—Move to Hopewell, New Jersey; son Charles is kidnapped, his body later found; son Jon is born August 16.

1933—Lindberghs seek European air routes for Pan American Airlines.

1934—Bruno Richard Hauptmann is arrested as a suspect in Lindbergh baby kidnapping.

1935—Hauptmann is found guilty of kidnapping and murder and condemned to death; Lindberghs move to England.

1936—Lindberghs are invited to Germany to survey airpower.

1937—Son Land is born May 12.

1938—Lindberghs move to Illiec Island in France.

1939—Return to the United States; World War II begins and Lindbergh opposes U.S. involvement.

1940—Daughter Anne is born October 2.

1941—Lindbergh testifies in Congress against Lend-Lease Bill to aid Great Britain during the war; joins isolationist organization, America First; the United States enters World War II.

1942—Son Scott is born August 13.

1942 —Lindbergh becomes technical consultant to
–1943 Ford Motor Company and United Aircraft Corporation.

1945—Daughter Reeve is born October 2.

1946—Lindbergh family moves to Darien, Connecticut.

1953—Lindbergh's book *The Spirit of St. Louis* becomes national best-seller.

1954—*The Spirit of St. Louis* wins the Pulitzer Prize for biography; death of mother, Evangeline Land Lindbergh.

1960s—Joins World Wildlife Fund and works for conservation and protection of endangered species.

1970—Publishes *The Wartime Journals of Charles A. Lindbergh.*

1973—Dedicates Lindbergh Interpretative Center in Little Falls, Minnesota.

1974—Dies of cancer, at age seventy-two, in Hawaii, August 26.

Chapter 1. A Pilot's Dream

1. Brendan Gill, *Lindbergh Alone* (New York: Harcourt Brace Jovanovich, 1977), p. 3.

2. Walter S. Ross, *The Last Hero: Charles A. Lindbergh* (New York: Harper & Row, 1976), p. 98.

3. Ibid., p. 107.

4. Kenneth S. Davis, *The Hero: Charles A. Lindbergh and the American Dream* (New York: Longmans, 1960), p. 189.

5. Ibid., p. 188.

6. Charles A. Lindbergh, *The Spirit of St. Louis* (New York: Charles Scribner's Sons, 1953), pp. 423–424.

Chapter 2. Boyhood—Farm and City

1. A. Scott Berg, *Lindbergh* (New York: G. P. Putnam's Sons, 1998), p. 29.

2. Ibid., p. 31.

3. Charles A. Lindbergh, *Autobiography of Values* (New York: Harcourt Brace Jovanovich, 1978), pp. 58–59.

4. Charles A. Lindbergh, *The Spirit of St. Louis* (New York: Charles Scribner's Sons, 1953), p. 245.

5. Joyce Milton, *Loss of Eden: A Biography of Charles and Anne Morrow Lindbergh* (New York: HarperCollins, 1993), pp. 20–21.

6. Ibid.

7. Walter S. Ross, *The Last Hero: Charles A. Lindbergh* (New York: Harper & Row, 1976), p. 31.

8. Berg, p. 43.

9. Lindbergh, *Autobiography of Values*, p. 55.

10. Kenneth S. Davis, *The Hero: Charles A. Lindbergh and the American Dream* (New York: Longmans, 1960), p. 16.

11. Ibid., pp. 56–57.

12. Ibid., p. 62.
13. Lindbergh, *The Spirit of St. Louis*, p. 376.
14. Leonard Mosley, *Lindbergh: A Biography* (New York: Doubleday, 1976), p. 12.
15. Berg, p. 45.
16. Charles A. Lindbergh, *Boyhood on the Upper Mississippi* (St. Paul: Minnesota Historical Society, 1972), p. 31.
17. Milton, p. 25.
18. Ibid.
19. Berg, p. 50.
20. Ibid.

Chapter 3. Eye on the Sky

1. Charles A. Lindbergh, *Autobiography of Values* (New York: Harcourt Brace Jovanovich, 1978), p. 62.
2. Ibid.
3. Charles A. Lindbergh, *"WE"* (New York: G. P. Putnam's Sons, 1927), p. 23.
4. Leonard Mosley, *Lindbergh: A Biography* (New York: Doubleday, 1976), p. 28.
5. Kenneth S. Davis, *The Hero: Charles A. Lindbergh and the American Dream* (New York: Longmans, 1960), p. 66.
6. Brendan Gill, *Lindbergh Alone* (New York: Harcourt Brace Jovanovich, 1977), p. 86.
7. Davis, p. 70.
8. Ibid., p. 69.
9. A. Scott Berg, *Lindbergh* (New York: G. P. Putnam's Sons, 1998), pp. 57–58.
10. Gill, pp. 86–87.
11. Walter S. Ross, *The Last Hero: Charles A. Lindbergh* (New York: Harper & Row, 1964), p. 43.
12. Ibid., p. 44.
13. Ibid., p. 46.
14. Davis, p. 79.
15. Ibid.
16. Ibid., p. 80.
17. Ibid., pp. 81–82.
18. Berg, p. 65.

19. Ibid.

20. Lindbergh, "*WE*," p. 28.

21. Berg, p. 66.

22. Ibid.

23. Joyce Milton, *Loss of Eden: A Biography of Charles and Anne Morrow Lindbergh* (New York: Harper Collins, 1993), p. 47.

24. Ibid.

25. Charles A.. Lindbergh, *The Spirit of St. Louis* (New York: Charles Scribner's Sons, 1953), pp. 267–268.

Chapter 4. Flying High

1. Walter S. Ross, *The Last Hero: Charles A. Lindbergh* (New York: Harper & Row, 1964), p. 53.

2. Ibid., pp. 53–54.

3. Charles A. Lindbergh, *"WE"* (New York: G. P. Putnam's Sons, 1927), p. 43.

4. Ibid., p. 53.

5. Ross, p. 55.

6. A. Scott Berg, *Lindbergh* (New York: G. P. Putnam's Sons, 1998), p. 71.

7. Lindbergh, p. 72.

8. Leonard Mosley, *Lindbergh: A Biography* (New York: Doubleday, 1976), p. 52.

9. Ross, p. 60.

10. Mosley, p. 54.

11. Ibid., pp. 55–56.

12. Kenneth S. Davis, *The Hero: Charles A. Lindbergh and the American Dream* (New York: Longmans, 1960), p. 105.

13. Joyce Milton, *Loss of Eden: A Biography of Charles and Anne Morrow Lindbergh* (New York: HarperCollins, 1993), pp. 60–61.

14. Charles A. Lindbergh, *Autobiography of Values* (New York: Harcourt Brace Jovanovich, 1978), p. 10.

15. Ibid., pp. 389–390.

16. Ibid., p. 390.

17. Davis, p. 114.

18. Ibid.

19. Berg, p. 79.
20. Milton, p. 67.
21. Davis, p. 129.
22. Lindbergh, *Autobiography of Values*, p. 67.
23. Ibid.
24. Lindbergh, *"WE,"* pp. 185–187.

Chapter 5. A Major Challenge

1. A. Scott Berg, *Lindbergh* (New York: G. P. Putnam's Sons, 1998), p. 91.

2. Ibid., p. 92.

3. Ibid.

4. Kenneth S. Davis, *The Hero: Charles A. Lindbergh and the American Dream* (New York: Longmans, 1960), p. 151.

5. Walter S. Ross, *The Last Hero: Charles A. Lindbergh* (New York: Harper & Row, 1976), p. 88.

6. Ibid., p, 89.

7. Ibid., pp. 89–91.

8. Berg, p. 100.

9. Brendan Gill, *Lindbergh Alone* (New York: Harcourt Brace Jovanovich, 1977), p. 24.

10. Ross, pp. 92–93.

11. Ibid., pp. 96–97.

12. Ibid. p. 98.

13. Leonard Mosley, *Lindbergh: A Biography* (New York: Doubleday, 1976), p. 91.

14. Berg, pp. 104–105.

15. Mosley, p. 92.

16. Joyce Milton, *Loss of Eden: A Biography of Charles and Anne Morrow Lindbergh* (New York: HarperCollins, 1993), p. 114.

17. Charles A. Lindbergh, *Autobiography of Values* (New York: Harcourt Brace Jovanovich, 1978), p. 77.

18. Ibid.

19. Peter Jennings, "The Century: Heaven and Earth," ABC NEWS, aired March 29, 1999. Transcript, pp. 9–10.

20. "Flight," *TIME, Special Anniversary Issue,* October 1983, p. 76.

21. Ross, p. 90.
22. Charles A. Lindbergh, *The Spirit of St. Louis* (New York: Charles Scribner's Sons, 1953), pp. 483–485.
23. Gill, p. 146.
24. Ibid., 147.

Chapter 6. Ambassador by Air

1. Brendan Gill, *Lindbergh Alone* (New York: Harcourt Brace Jovanovich, 1977), p. 161.
2. A. Scott Berg, *Lindbergh* (New York: G. P. Putnam's Sons, 1998), p. 154.
3. Charles A. Lindbergh, *"WE"* (New York: G. P. Putnam's Sons, 1927), p. 280.
4. Ibid., pp. 281–285.
5. Walter S. Ross, *The Last Hero: Charles A. Lindbergh* (New York: Harper & Row, 1976), p. 135.
6. Ibid., pp. 136–137.
7. Ibid., p. 137.
8. Kenneth S. Davis, *The Hero: Charles A. Lindbergh and the American Dream* (New York: Longmans, 1960), p. 234.
9. Gill, pp. 167–170.
10. Berg, p. 166.
11. Davis, p. 235.
12. Ross, p. 143.
13. Michael Parfit, "Retracing Lindy's Victorious Trip Across the Country," *Smithsonian*, October 1987, p. 203.
14. Ibid., pp. 208–210.
15. Berg, pp. 168–169.
16. Ross, p. 160.
17. Charles A. Lindbergh, *Autobiography of Values* (New York: Harcourt Brace Jovanovich, 1978), p. 83.
18. Ibid., pp. 87–88.
19. Ross, p. 166.
20. Anne Morrow Lindbergh, *Bring Me a Unicorn* (New York: Harcourt Brace Jovanovich, 1971), p. 108.
21. Berg, p. 175.
22. Ibid., pp. 174–175.

23. Davis, p. 265.

24. Ibid.

Chapter 7. The Pilot and His Mate

1. Walter S. Ross, *The Last Hero: Charles A. Lindbergh* (New York: Harper & Row, 1976), pp. 172–173.

2. Joyce Milton, *Loss of Eden: A Biography of Charles and Anne Morrow Lindbergh* (New York: HarperCollins, 1993). p. 175.

3. Charles A. Lindbergh, *Autobiography of Values* (New York: Harcourt Brace Jovanovich, 1978), p. 117.

4. Ibid., p. 119.

5. Anne Morrow Lindbergh, *Bring Me a Unicorn* (New York: Harcourt Brace Jovanovich, 1971), p. 191.

6. Ibid., p. 182.

7. Dorothy Herrmann, *Anne Morrow Lindbergh: A Gift for Life* (New York: Ticknor and Fields, 1992), p. 50.

8. Milton, p. 178.

9. Anne Morrow Lindbergh, *Hour of Gold, Hour of Lead: Diaries and Letters, 1929–1932* (New York: Harcourt Brace Jovanovich, 1973) p. 127.

10. Ross, p. 182.

11. Anne Morrow Lindbergh, *Hour of Gold, Hour of Lead*, p. 138.

12. Charles A. Lindbergh, *Autobiography of Values*, pp. 131–133.

13. Jean Adams and Margaret Kimball, *Heroines of the Sky* (New York: Doubleday Doran, 1942), p. 228.

14. Anne Morrow Lindbergh, *North to the Orient* (New York: Harcourt Brace, 1935), p. 61.

15. Anne Morrow Lindbergh, *Hour of Gold, Hour of Lead*, p. 192.

Chapter 8. Tragedy at Home

1. Anne Morrow Lindbergh, *Hour of Gold, Hour of Lead: Diaries and Letters, 1929–1932* (New York: Harcourt Brace Jovanovich, 1973), p. 204.

2. Dorothy Herrmann, *Anne Morrow Lindbergh: A Gift for Life* (New York: Ticknor and Fields, 1992), p. 67.

3. Walter S. Ross, *The Last Hero: Charles A. Lindbergh* (New York: Harper & Row, 1976), p. 196.

4. Ibid., p. 197.

5. Leonard Mosley, *Lindbergh: A Biography* (New York: Doubleday, 1976), pp. 162–163.

6. Kenneth Davis, *The Hero: Charles A. Lindbergh and the American Dream* (New York: Longmans, 1960), p. 319.

7. Ibid., p. 321.

8. Mosley, pp. 164–165.

9. Joyce Milton, *Loss of Eden: A Biography of Charles and Anne Morrow Lindbergh* (New York: Harper Collins, 1993), p. 250.

10. Mosley, p. 170.

11. Ibid.

12. A. Scott Berg, *Lindbergh* (G. P. Putnam's Sons, 1998), pp. 281–282.

13. Ibid., p. 286.

14. Anne Morrow Lindbergh, *Locked Rooms and Open Doors: Diaries and Letters, 1933–1935* (New York: Harcourt Brace Jovanovich, 1974), pp. 188–189.

15. Mosley, pp. 178–180.

16. Davis, p. 338.

17. Joan Saunders Wixen, "I Covered the Lindbergh Kidnapping," *Modern Maturity*, April/May 1982, p. 38.

18. Berg, pp. 303–304.

19. Davis, pp. 354–357.

20. Charles A. Lindbergh, *Autobiography of Values* (New York: Harcourt Brace Jovanovich, 1978), p. 144.

21. Berg, pp. 340–341.

Chapter 9. Sunshine and Shadows

1. Dorothy Herrmann, *Anne Morrow Lindbergh: A Gift for Life* (New York: Ticknor and Fields, 1992), pp. 162–163.

2. Tom D. Crouch, "Reaching Toward Space," *Smithsonian*, February 2000, pp. 38–42.

3. Joyce Milton, *Loss of Eden: A Biography of Charles and Anne Morrow Lindbergh* (New York: HarperCollins, 1993), p. 339.

4. Herrmann, pp. 176–177.

5. Walter S. Ross, *The Last Hero: Charles A. Lindbergh* (New York: Harper & Row, 1976), pp. 264–265.

6. Ibid., p. 266.

7. Ibid.

8. Herrmann, pp. 187–188.

9. A. Scott Berg, *Lindbergh* (New York: G. P. Putnam's Sons, 1998), p. 357.

10. Ross, p. 276.

11. Ibid., pp. 234–235.

12. Ibid., pp. 279–280.

13. Herrmann, p. 210.

14. Anne Morrow Lindbergh, *The Flower and the Nettle: Diaries and Letters, 1936–1939* (New York: Harcourt Brace Jovanovich, 1976), p, 391.

15. Berg, p. 387.

16. Herrmann, pp. 220–221.

17. Ibid., p. 221.

18. Charles A. Lindbergh, "Aviation, Geography and Race," *Reader's Digest*, November 1939, cited at <http://members.core.com/nordic/lindbergh.htm> (June 29, 2001).

19. Leonard Mosley, *Lindbergh: A Biography* (New York: Doubleday, 1976), p. 275.

20. Berg, pp. 361–362.

21. Ibid.

22. Berg, p. 408.

23. Wayne S. Cole, *Charles A. Lindbergh and the Battle Against American Intervention in World War II* (New York: Harcourt Brace Jovanovich, 1974), p. 93.

24. Herrmann, pp. 222–223.

25. Mosley, p. 277.

26. Ross, pp. 310–311.

27. Ibid., p. 312.

28. Ibid.

29. Ibid., p. 314.

30. James Cross Giblin, *Charles A. Lindbergh: A Human Hero* (New York: Clarion Books, 1997), pp. 182–184.

31. Cole, p. 209.

Chapter 10. America at War

1. Kenneth S. Davis, *The Hero: Charles A. Lindbergh and the American Dream* (New York: Longmans, 1960), p. 416.

2. Wayne S. Cole, *Charles A. Lindbergh and the Battle Against American Intervention in World War II* (New York: Harcourt Brace Jovanovich, 1974), p. 221.

3. Joyce Milton, *Loss of Eden: A Biography of Charles and Anne Morrow Lindbergh* (New York: Harper Collins, 1993), p. 408.

4. Charles A. Lindbergh, *The Wartime Journals of Charles A. Lindbergh* (New York: Harcourt Brace Jovanovich, 1970), p. 726.

5. Davis, p. 420.

6. Cole, p. 223.

7. Lindbergh, p. 1011.

8. Richard C. Kirkland, *Tales of a War Pilot* (Washington: Smithsonian Institution Press, 1999), pp. 24–26.

9. Cole, p. 223.

10. Milton, pp. 411–412.

11. Cole, pp. 223–224.

12. Walter S. Ross, *The Last Hero: Charles A. Lindbergh* (New York: Harper and Row, 1976), p. 332.

13. Lindbergh, p. xiv.

14. Milton, p. 416.

15. Lindbergh, p. 996.

16. A. Scott Berg, *Lindbergh* (New York, G. P. Putnam's Sons, 1998), pp. 474–476.

17. Ibid., p. 476.

18. Ibid., p. 487.

19. Ibid.

20. Anne Morrow Lindbergh, *War Within and Without: Diaries and Letters, 1939–1944* (New York: Harcourt Brace Jovanovich, 1980), p. xxix.

Chapter 11. Family and Home
1. A. Scott Berg, *Lindbergh* (New York: G. P. Putnam's Sons, 1998), pp. 478–479.

2. Ibid., 480.

3. Reeve Lindbergh, *Under a Wing* (New York: Simon & Schuster, 1998), p. 77.

4. Walter S. Ross, *The Last Hero: Charles A. Lindbergh* (New York: Harper & Row, 1976), pp. 336–337.

5. Berg, p. 485.

6. Charles A. Lindbergh, *The Spirit of St. Louis* (New York: Charles Scribner's Sons, 1953), p. v.

7. Leonard Mosley, *Lindbergh: A Biography* (New York: Doubleday, 1976), p. 350.

8. Berg, p. 490.

9. Ibid., pp. 498–499.

10. Mosley, p. 359.

Chapter 12. Back to Earth
1. "Concorde—Last Flight of the Swan," *Chicago Tribune*, August 26, 2000, sec. 1, p. 10.

2. Leonard Mosley, *Lindbergh: A Biography* (New York: Doubleday, 1976), p. 366.

3. Anne Morrow Lindbergh, *Earth Shine* (New York: Harcourt, Brace & World, 1966), pp. 53–58.

4. A. Scott Berg, *Lindbergh* (New York: G. P. Putnam's Sons, 1998), pp. 526–527.

5. Joyce Milton, *Loss of Eden: A Biography of Charles and Anne Morrow Lindbergh* (New York: HarperCollins, 1993), pp. 452–453.

6. Ibid., p. 462.

7. Ibid., p. 451

8. Berg, p. 537.

9. Charles A. Lindbergh, *The Wartime Journals of Charles A. Lindbergh* (New York: Harcourt Brace Jovanovich, 1970), p. xii.

10. Berg, pp. 545–546.

11. Ibid., p. 547.

12. Dorothy Herrmann, *Anne Morrow Lindbergh: A Gift for Life* (New York: Ticknor and Fields, 1992), p. 315.

13. Rudolph Chelminski, "The Lindberghs Liberate Monkeys from Constraints," *Smithsonian,* March 1977, pp. 59–64.

14. Susan Hertog, *Anne Morrow Lindbergh* (New York: Doubleday, 1999), p. 481.

15. T. Willard Hunter, *The Spirit of Charles Lindbergh* (Lanham, Md.: Madison Books, 1993), pp. 142–143.

16. Milton, pp. 471–472.

17. Reeve Lindbergh, "Heroes and Icons of the 20th Century," *Time,* June 14, 1999, pp. 75–76.

Berg, A. Scott. *Lindbergh.* New York: G. P. Putnam's Sons, 1998.

Davis, Kenneth S. *The Hero: Charles A. Lindbergh and the American Dream.* New York: Doubleday & Company, 1959.

Giblin, James Cross. *Charles A. Lindbergh: A Human Hero.* New York: Clarion Books, 1997.

Gill, Brendan. *Lindbergh Alone.* New York: Harcourt Brace Jovanovich, 1977.

Lindbergh, Anne Morrow. *North to the Orient.* New York: Harcourt, Brace, and Company, 1935.

———. *Hour of Gold, Hour of Lead: Diaries and Letters of Anne Morrow Lindbergh, 1929–1932.* New York: Harcourt Brace Jovanovich, 1973.

———. *War Within and Without: Diaries and Letters of Anne Morrow Lindbergh, 1939–1944.* New York: Harcourt Brace Jovanovich, 1980.

Lindbergh, Charles A. *"WE."* New York: G. P. Putnam's Sons, 1927.

———. *The Spirit of St. Louis.* New York: Charles Scribner's Sons, 1953.

———. *The Wartime Journals of Charles A. Lindbergh.* New York: Harcourt Brace Jovanovich, 1970.

———. *Autobiography of Values.* New York: Harcourt Brace Jovanovich, 1978.

Lindbergh, Reeve. *Under a Wing: A Memoir.* New York: Simon & Schuster, 1998.

Milton, Joyce. *Loss of Eden: A Biography of Charles and Anne Morrow Lindbergh.* New York: HarperCollins, 1993.

Mosley, Leonard. *Lindbergh: A Biography.* New York: Doubleday, 1976.

Ross, Walter S. *The Last Hero: Charles A. Lindbergh.* New York: Harper & Row, 1976.

Internet Addresses

World Book Encyclopedia
<http://www2.worldbook.com/features/features.asp?feature=aviators&page=html/av2.htm&direct=yes>

The PBS American Experience site
<http://www.pbs.org/wgbh/amex/lindbergh/>

Gander Academy Web Resources for Students
<http://www.stemnet.nf.ca/CITE/lindy.htm>

National Aviation Hall of Fame site
<http://www.nationalaviation.org/enshrinee/lindberghch.html>

Index

Page numbers for photographs are in **boldface** type.